teach yourself...

C++

AI STEVENS

PRESS

A Subsidiary of
Henry Holt and Co., Inc.

Copyright © 1991 by Management Information Source, Inc.
a subsidiary of Henry Holt and Company, Inc.
115 West 18th Street
New York, New York 10011

Second Edition—1991

ISBN 1-55828-176-2

Printed in the United States of America
10   9   8   7   6   5   4   3   2

MIS:Press books are available at special discounts for bulk purchases for sales promotions, premiums,
fund-raising, or educational use. Special editions or book excerpts can also be created to specification.

For details contact: Special Sales Director
                          MIS:Press
                          a subsidiary of Henry Holt and Company, Inc.
                          115 West 18th Street
                          New York, New York 10011

TRADEMARKS

Borland C++ is a trademark of Borland International, Inc.
Comeau C++ is a trademark of Comeau Computing
MS-DOS is a trademark of Microsoft Corporation
TopSpeed C++ is a trademark of Jensen & Partners, Inc.
UNIX is a trademark of AT&T Bell Laboratories
Zortech C++ is a trademark of Zortech Limited

Dedication

To the memory of Charlie Robb

Acknowledgements

Thanks to:

Borland International for the Borland C++ compiler
Comeau Computing for Comeau C++
Jensen & Partners, Inc., for the TopSpeed C++ compiler
Zortech for the Zortech 2.1 C++ compiler.

Contents

Contents

Contents

Contents

Preface

This book is the second edition of Teach Yourself C++, a tutorial text with which you, a C programmer, can teach yourself C++. Since the first edition was published a year ago, several changes have occurred in C++. AT&T's Version 2.1, which introduced a number of improvements to the language, has become the accepted version. Many new C++ programming environments have emerged, including several that run in the MS-DOS environment. The ANSI X3J16 committee has formed and is developing a standard definition of C++. Bjarne Stroustrup, the creator of the C++ language, published the Annotated C++ Reference Manual with coauthor Margaret A. Ellis. That book is the definitive work on C++ and is the base document from which the X3J16 committee is working.

You will learn C++ in this book the same way thousands of C programmers did with the first edition—in the same sequence that I learned C++ before I wrote the first book, except that you will have help. I waded through a lot of heavy stuff, most of which I could not understand, as I tried to learn this language. From that experience I developed what I believe to be the correct sequence of learning steps that a C programmer must take to learn and use the features of C++. With this book as a guide and your future in hand, you can take those same steps without all the false turns and confusion that confront the unwary newcomer who tries to go it alone.

Most of the exercises in this book will compile and run with any version 2.0 or higher implementation of C++. The Borland C++ 2.0 and Zortech C++ 2.1 compilers were the basis for the development of the exercise programs. Subsequently, I compiled the exercises with TopSpeed C++ and Comeau C++. The Zortech implementation has a number of departures from the language, and some of the exercises do not work or compile properly when used with Zortech C++. The book includes comments to that effect where it applies. None of the exercises are specific to the PC/AT platform or the Borland and Zortech extensions to the language, libraries, or classes.

Introduction

This book enables you, as a C programmer, to teach yourself the C++ programming language. C++ is a superset of the C language, containing all of the program constructs of C, therefore the C programmer already has a head start on the learning process. This new language adds extensions to C that improve its syntax, expand its application, and bring to it some of the features of object-oriented programming.

teach yourself... C++ leads you through the learning process with a series of exercises. Each exercise includes C++ source code that you can compile and execute. To get the maximum benefit from these lessons, you should have a programmer's editor and a C++ compiler or translator program with which to practice.

Introduction

The C++ exercises in this book lead you through the subjects related to C++ in a sequence that introduces simpler concepts first, and then uses them in subsequent exercises where gradually more complex subjects are developed. These exercises often build upon the ones that precede them, and you will frequently modify programs that you built in earlier exercises. Therefore, it is important that you follow the exercises in the order in which they appear. This book is a tutorial designed to help you teach the C++ programming language to yourself. It is not a language reference manual.

A complex subject such as a programming language often requires you to go into a learning loop. You cannot learn a lesson without knowing about a prerequisite lesson, which itself has the new lesson as a prerequisite. A case in point is the C++ standard input/output streams. To fully comprehend their syntax, you must know about C++ classes and overloaded operators, both of which are advanced topics in the hallowed halls of C++ learning. Yet to progress to where you can learn those advanced topics, you need to walk through an orderly sequence of program exercises that use the keyboard and screen, devices that are in the exclusive domain of input/output streams. What choice do you have but to use the **cin** and **cout** objects of the **istream** and **ostream** classes with a blind acceptance that what they do will eventually make sense? Trust the book and be patient — everything will eventually become clear. Stick with it, and you will be rewarded.

Because of this circular approach, the programmer who is already well versed in C++ might well find things to criticize in this book. Some exercises do not include code constructs that a seasoned C++ programmer would recognize as conventional, appropriate, or even downright necessary. These omissions are intentional and are because of the sequence of learning that is built into *teach yourself... C++*. Eventually the book will cover those bases. Other omissions are due to the highly advanced nature of C++ and the kind of strange and exotic code that it permits. There are elements in C++, just as in C, that a tutorial work should spare the newcomer. Later, when you have the language well in hand, you can push it to its limits.

The exercise programs in *teach yourself... C++* are small. They do not pretend to be full-blown, useful programs that you will take out into the workplace. The purpose of each exercise is to demonstrate the behavior of a particular feature of C++. Some of the exercises have the potential to grow into useful software tools, and you should view all of them with this possibility in mind. The strength of extensible programming languages such as C and C++ lies in their potential for the programmer to build reusable software

2

tools. You will soon learn that C++, far more than C and most other traditional programming languages, readily adapts itself to that potential.

Most exercises in this book are complete programs that you can enter, compile, and execute. A few exercises illustrate common programming errors and might not compile or run properly. Where this is true, the book and the comments in the code clearly point it out. Some programs consist of the combined code from several exercises. Where this happens, the dependent code always follows closely behind the code it needs. You will have no trouble keeping track of where you are if you follow the exercises in the order in which they appear.

A Brief History of C++

The C++ programming language was designed and originally developed by Bjarne Stroustrup in the Computer Science Research Center at AT&T Bell Labs in Murray Hill, New Jersey. He began this work in about 1980 in answer to a need for a simulation language that had the features of object-oriented programming, then a relatively new programming paradigm. Rather than design a new language from the ground up, Dr. Stroustrup decided to add the features he wanted to the well-established C language, itself an earlier development from within the Center.

C was already implemented on several different architectures, and it already had the property of supporting portable-program development, so Dr. Stroustrup made an historic decision: He elected to develop the C++ language system as a translator program that processes C++ source language into C source language. The translated C source language could then be compiled on any computer system that supports C. He called his translator program CFRONT, and most implementations of C++ have been ports of that same CFRONT program and its successors, the source code of which is available to language system developers under license from AT&T. The C++ language has been available outside of AT&T since about 1985.

Over the years, C++ has continued through several versions, with the latest being version 2.1. Dr. Stroustrup remains its staunchest advocate and is a strong contributing presence wherever C++ issues surface. With the standardization of C now completed by the ANSI X3J11 committee, a new committee, X3J16, was formed to tackle the formidable task of defining a standard for C++.

The C++ Legacy to C Programmers

Even if you have never seen a C++ program, you have been touched by it. Although C came before C++, many of the features in C today saw their first light of day in the improvements that Dr. Stroustrup sought to add to the language when he defined his superset. These features were widely admired, were incorporated into various C compilers, and were ultimately adopted by the ANSI X3J11 committee as parts of standard C.

Examples of the C++ improvements that are now standard in C are function prototypes, void, and the **const** type-specifier.

Learning C++

C++, like C before it, is becoming the language of choice among programmers. As this book is being written, C++ language systems are appearing in every environment and on most architectures where C once reigned supreme, adding testimony to the assertion of Dr. Stroustrup and others that C++ will ultimately replace C. It therefore behooves the rest of us to learn this new technique.

The best way for a C programmer to learn C++ is to take it a small step at a time, trying its various features in a sequence that introduces small portions of the C++ extensions. Remember, with a C++ compiler, you can still build a C program. The full range of C language features and C standard-library functions is automatically a part of every C++ language system because C++, as originally designed, passes through to a C compiler. So you can begin with the C that you already know and gradually add the enhancements of C++, learning a little bit at a time.

The Organization of this Book

Chapters 1 through 10 are the lessons and exercises that you will use to teach yourself C++. The lessons begin with an elementary introduction to the extensions that C++ brings to C and proceed through to the more complex features of the language.

A glossary and bibliography follow Chapter 10. The glossary provides brief definitions of terms that are common to C++. The bibliography lists the books and articles that contributed to the research that went into this book. As such, it constitutes a reasonable library for the C++ programmer.

The C++ programming language operates in many environments on many platforms. Some of the implementations are ports of the AT&T CFRONT translator program; others are complete compiler systems with integrated editors, debuggers, and linkers. To avoid confusion, this book will refer to all such implementations as C++ compilers.

Chapter 1

C++ Basics

C++ is is the C language with extensions and improvements. Extensions are new features in the language; while improvements are better ways of doing the things that C already does. You will teach yourself C++ by gathering those improvements and extensions into your programming vocabulary as additions to what you can do as a C programmer. Later, you will apply this new knowledge to the development of systems that employ the object-oriented features of C++. This chapter is your first step toward that goal.

Exercise 1-1 shows you the smallest possible C++ program.

```
main()
{
}
```

Exercise 1-1 — The Simplest C++ Program.

Look familiar? It should. It's the smallest possible C program as well. Because C++ is a superset of the C language, you can use a C++ compiler to develop and compile C programs. The minimum program just shown does not do anything, of course. It contains no more than the one required function, which, as in C, must be named **main**.

Exercise 1-2 presents a program that does something.

```
#include <iostream.h>

main()
{
    cout << "Hello, world";
}
```

Exercise 1-2 — Hello.cpp.

This program is *hello.cpp*, the C++ equivalent to the *hello.c* program that introduced the world to the C language in Kernighan and Ritchie's *The C Programming Language*. But instead of *stdio.h*, the program includes *iostream.h*, and instead of a **printf** call, it uses an unfamiliar syntax with the undefined variable name **cout**, the bitwise shift left operator (<<), and, the only familiar part of the example, a string that greets the world. You might well wonder about the meaning of it all.

Standard Streams

The *hello.cpp* program in Exercise 1-2 is your introduction to the powerful C++ facility called the **class**, a feature that lets a programmer define new data types and operators. This is too early in your lessons for a complete explanation of the **class**, but you do need to know that the designers of C++ used its features to develop an improved stream input/ output system. That design has become a standard in C++ programs, and because you will be using these improved streams to read and display information throughout these lessons, you need this somewhat premature exposure to it.

The **cout** variable, seen in Exercise 1-2, is the C++ standard output stream, which writes to the console:

```
cout << "Hello, world";
```

In Exercise 1-2, the string "Hello, world" is sent to the standard output device stream. The << operator is the output operator. It points from what is being sent to where it is going. In this example, the string is going to the **cout** device.

Suppose you wanted to display the contents of an integer variable on the screen. In C you would use the **printf** function along with a format string that describes the parameters to **printf** like the following:

```
printf("%d", amount);
```

Exercise 1-3 illustrates how the C++ stream output devices do not need a format string to describe the data types that are to be displayed.

```
#include <iostream.h>

main()
{
    int amount = 123;
    cout << amount;
}
```

Exercise 1-3 — The Standard Output Stream.

In Exercise 1-3, you displayed an integer value on the console. Suppose you wanted to display the value as part of a sentence. By using the techniques learned in Exercise 1-3, you can display different data types by sending each of them in turn to the output stream. The **cout** stream can discern the format of the data type because the C++ compiler figures it out when it compiles your code. The discussions in Chapters 4 and 8 on function and operator overloading will show you how the compiler does this. For now you can accept it as a feature of the standard output stream in C++. Ready or not, you should try to acquaint yourself with the stream input/output facility, because you need it to display the results of your work on the screen.

Exercise 1-4 illustrates how to send a string, an integer, and a character constant to the output stream.

```
#include <iostream.h>

main()
{
    int amount = 123;
    cout << "The value of amount is ";
    cout << amount;
    cout << '.';
}
```

Exercise 1-4 — Multiple Data Type to the Standard Output Stream.

Exercise 1-4 displays the following message on the screen:

```
The value of amount is 123.
```

The exercise sends three different data types to **cout**, a string literal, the integer **amount** variable, and a character-constant '.' to add the period punctuation to the sentence. This exercise might, however, send you racing back to the standard C language **printf** function, because the exercise used three statements where **printf** could have done it in one.

Exercise 1-5 is an example of how you can use the C++ **cout** stream to send multiple data types to the standard output stream with what appears to be one statement. The displayed value is the same one that Exercise 1-4 delivers.

```
#include <iostream.h>

main()
{
    int amount = 123;
    cout << "The value of amount is " << amount << '.';
}
```

Exercise 1-5 — Several Outputs in One Statement.

In Exercise 1-5, several data types are tacked together by repeating the << operator and the data type. This behavior is a by-product of the **this** pointer (which is used in the definition of the stream class and that gets full treatment in Chapter 7). For now, accept the behavior and forge ahead.

Formatted Output

One deficiency in the way you have used **cout** so far is that it does not show support for the well-formatted displays of the C **printf** family of functions. Suppose you want to display the hexadecimal representation of a variable, for example. The C **printf** function handles that nicely. How does C++ do it?

> Whenever you ask yourself how can you can get C++ to do something that C does, remember that the entire C language dwells inside of C++. In the absence of a better way, revert to C. It will work nicely. Until **cout** and its ilk are second nature to you, for example, simply use **printf**.

C++ associates a set of manipulators with the output stream that changes the default format for integer arguments. You insert the manipulators into the stream to make the change. The manipulators' symbolic values are **dec**, **oct**, and **hex**.

Exercise 1-6 shows how you can display an integer value in its three possible configurations.

```
#include <iostream.h>

main()
{
    int amount = 123;
    cout << dec << amount << ' ' << oct << amount << ' '
         << hex << amount;
}
```

Exercise 1-6 — Formatting Numerical Data.

The exercise inserts each of the manipulators (**dec** , **oct** , and **hex**) to convert the value in **amount** into different representations.

Exercise 1-6 displays the following result:

`123 173 7b`

Each of the values shown is a different representation of the decimal value 123, which the exercise initializes into the **amount** variable before displaying it.

> Note that the Zortech 2.1 compiler does not support these stream manipulators.

The Standard Error Stream

C++ uses the **cerr** object with the same syntax that it uses for **cout** , with the exception that **cerr** sends its output to the standard error device. This technique allows you to send error messages and such to the console from programs that could have the standard output device redirected to another file or device.

The Standard Input Stream

Now that you can display all kinds of data on the screen, you will want to read some data into your programs as well. C++ includes its own version of standard input in the **cin** object.

Exercise 1-7 shows you how to use **cin** to read an integer from the keyboard.

```
#include <iostream.h>

main()
{
    int amount;
    cout << "Enter an amount...";
    cin >> amount;
    cout << "The amount you entered was " << amount;
}
```

Exercise 1-7 — The Standard Input Stream.

The exercise prompts you to enter an amount by sending the prompting string to **cout**. The **cin** device sends the value that you enter to the **amount** integer variable. The next statement displays the amount on **cout** as a way of demonstrating that the **cin** operation worked.

Exercise 1-7 displays the following messages. The first "123" is the amount you would type into the program.

```
Enter an amount...123
The amount you entered was 123
```

Assume for the moment that you are using this program in a system where the integer occupies 16 bits. Observe that if you enter the value 65535, the displayed value is –1. If you enter 65536, the value is 0. This effect is because the **amount** variable is a signed integer. Try changing the type to an unsigned integer. Try entering a value with decimal places.

The **cin** device works with strings as well.

Exercise 1-8 shows you how the **cin** device can be used to read a string value from the keyboard.

```
#include <iostream.h>

main()
{
    char name[20];
    cout << "Enter a name...";
    cin >> name;
    cout << "The name you entered was " << name;
}
```

Exercise 1-8 — Reading a String.

Exercise 1-8 displays the following messages. The name "Tyler" is the name you would type into the program.

```
Enter a name...Tyler
The name you entered was Tyler
```

The approach shown in Exercise 1-8 has a flaw. The character array is only 20 characters long. If you type too many characters, you will overflow the stack and peculiar things will happen. The **get** function solves this problem. You will learn about **get** in Chapter 10, Advanced C++ Input/Output Streams. For now, the exercises will assume that you will not type more characters than a **cin** string can accept.

It is important for you to know that **cin** and **cout** are not a part of the compiled C++ language as such. They are not built-in data types, and the << and >> operators are not, in this context, built-in C++ operators that the designers installed into the language. The input and output streams are implemented as C++ classes, and **cin** and **cout** are instances of those classes. This implementation exists outside the C++ compiler system itself, just as the **printf** and **scanf** functions are implemented through functions in the C language and not as a part of the C compiler. But where C limits its extensibility to function and structure definitions, C++ allows you to define new data types and to associate custom operators with those data types. You will learn how to do this later.

C++ Comments

The exercises so far have been small, and they have had no comments. C++ supports the C comment format where the /* character sequence begins a comment and the */ sequence ends it. But C++ has another comment format, one that is preferred by many programmers, and some C compilers are adopting it as well. The C++ comment token is the double-slash (//) sequence. Wherever this sequence appears (other than inside a string), everything to the end of the current line is a comment.

Exercise 1-9 repeats Exercise 1-8 and adds comments to the program.

```
#include <iostream.h>

main()
{
    char name[20];              // declare a name string
    cout << "Enter a name...";  // request a name
    cin >> name;                // read the name
    // ------------ display the name
    cout << "The name you entered was " << name;
}
```

Exercise 1-9 — C++ Comments.

Prototypes

Standard C supports the use of function-declaration blocks that describe the function's class, return value, and parameters to the C compiler. This feature, called the function prototype, allows the compiler to check the function as coded against its prototype and to check all calls to the function for compliance with the prototype. C compilers do not require that a function be described in a prototype. If you provide a prototype, then the C compiler will insist that the rest of the code complies with it, but if you leave it out, at best you will get a warning.

C++ requires that all functions have prototypes. This requirement supports the implementation of overloaded functions which you will encounter in Chapter 4.

Exercise 1-10 uses a function named **display** to display the "Hello, world" message on the screen.

```
#include <iostream.h>

main()
{
    display("Hello, world");
}

display(char *s)
{
    cout << s;
}
```

Exercise 1-10 — A Program without Function Prototypes.

Because the **display** function has no prototype, the program in Exercise 1-10 will not pass the syntax-checking phase of the C++ compiler.

Exercise 1-11 adds a function prototype to the program in Exercise 1-10. This addition allows the program to compile without errors.

```
#include <iostream.h>

void display(char *s);

main()
{
    display("Hello, world");
}

void display(char *s)
{
    cout << s;
}
```

Exercise 1-11 — A Program with a Function Prototype.

Now, with a proper prototype, the program compiles and runs correctly. C++ requires, too, that functions be declared with C's new-style function declaration blocks where you declare the types of all parameters within the parentheses that follow the function's name. This convention, along with the prototype, is an innovation that C++ pioneered out of need and that the developers of the C language standard definition adopted, mainly because it is a good addition to the language. To preserve the integrity of older code, however, standard C allows a C program to use either convention for function declarations. Because C++ uses a stronger parameter type-checking system than C, however, C++ does not accept the older style.

The prototype and function-declaration requirements are strict but necessary ones. They represent exceptions to the general rule that a C++ compiler can handle a C program. If your C programs do not have function prototypes and new-style function-declaration blocks, then you must add those features before compiling the programs with a C++ compiler.

C++ Keywords

There is another issue to consider if you plan to port some C programs to C++. The C++ language necessarily adds key words to the lexicon. Key words have meaning to the language, and you must not use them for the names of variables. When you write C++ programs or convert C programs to C++, you must avoid the use of these words except in the ways intended in a C++ program. Naturally, C++ uses all the C key words. Here is the list of other key words that are new to C++:

asm	private
catch	protected
class	public
delete	template
friend	this
inline	throw
new	try
operator	virtual

You will learn the meaning of these key words by the time you have finished this book. Four of the words, **catch**, **template**, **throw**, and **try** are not a part of the language as this book is being written. They are being reserved now for use in experimental features not yet in general use. Chapter 11 discusses them. The **asm** key word is implementation-dependent and is not addressed in this book.

Summary

This chapter has given you a small taste of the C++ language. Its main purpose is to show you how the C++ input/output streams work so that you can use them in the exercises that follow. Chapter 2 will discuss some of the improvements that C++ brings to the C language. These improvements are not necessarily associated with the object-oriented programming paradigm, but do improve the way the C language works.

Chapter 2

C++ Extensions to C

C++ has often been described by programmers as an improved C. In many ways that is true because C++ offers the C programmer many better ways to write code within the structure of the C language. You already learned one of those improvements in Chapter 1. Many programmers prefer the C++ double-slash (//) comment style to the /* and */ tokens of C.

This chapter introduces several other improvements that C++ brings to the C programmer. These improvements enhance your use of the C language and prepare you for the more advanced object-oriented properties of C++. You will learn about default function arguments, variable declaration placement, the global scope resolution operator, and inline functions.

Default Function Arguments

A C++ function prototype can declare that some of the function's parameters have default values. If you omit the corresponding arguments when you call the function, the compiler inserts the default values where it expects to see the argument.

You can declare default values for arguments in a C++ function prototype in the following way:

```
void myfunc(int = 5, double = 1.23);
```

The expressions declare default values for the arguments. The C++ compiler substitutes the default values if you omit the arguments when you call the function. You can call the function by using any of the following ways:

```
myfunc(12, 3.45); // overrides both defaults
myfunc(3);        // effectively func(3, 1.23);
myfunc();         // effectively func(5, 1.23);
```

To omit the first parameter in these examples, you must omit the second one; however, you can omit the second parameter by itself. This rule applies to any number of parameters. You cannot omit a parameter unless you omit all the parameters to its right.

Exercise 2-1 is an example of the use of default parameters.

```
#include <iostream.h>

void show(int = 1, float = 2.3, long = 4);

main()
{
    show();                 // all three parameters default
    show(5);                // provide 1st parameter
    show(6, 7.8);           // provide 1st two
    show(9, 10.11, 12L);    // provide all three parameters
}

void show(int first, float second, long third)
{
    cout << "\nfirst = "  << first;
    cout << ", second = " << second;
    cout << ", third = "  << third;
}
```

Exercise 2-1 — A Program with Default Parameters in a Function Prototype.

Exercise 2-1, when you run it, displays the following result:

```
first = 1, second = 2.3, third = 4
first = 5, second = 2.3, third = 4
first = 6, second = 7.8, third = 4
first = 9, second = 10.11, third = 12
```

The first call to the **show** function in Exercise 2-1 allows the C++ compiler to provide the default values for the parameters as the prototype specifies them. The second call provides the first parameter and allows the compiler to provide the other two. The third call provides the first two and allows the compiler to provide the last. The fourth call provides all three parameters, and none of the defaults are used.

Variable Declaration Placement

In C, you must declare all variables at the beginning of the block in which they have scope. You may not intermix variable declaration and procedural expressions. C++ removes that restriction, allowing you to declare a variable anywhere before you reference it. This feature allows you to code the declaration of a variable closer to the code that uses it. When the declaration of a variable is near the code that uses it, the code becomes more readable. When you can see the variable's declaration in close proximity to its use, its purpose and behavior are easier to understand.

Exercise 2-2 shows you how you can relocate the declaration of a variable closer to its first reference.

```
#include <iostream.h>

main()
{
    cout << "Enter a number: ";
    int n;
    cin >> n;
    cout << "The number is: " << n;
}
```

Exercise 2-2 — Relocating a Variable Declaration.

Exercise 2-2 displays the following messages on the screen. The 234 is the number you enter.

```
Enter a number: 234
The number is: 234
```

The freedom to declare a variable anywhere in a block makes expressions such as the following one possible:

```
for(int ctr = Ø; ctr < MAXCTR; ctr++)
    // ...
```

Exercise 2-3 illustrates the use of declaring a variable in a block.

```
#include <iostream.h>

main()
{
    for (int lineno = 0; lineno < 5; lineno++)
        cout << "\nThis is line number: " << lineno;
}
```

Exercise 2-3 — Variable Declaration Placement.

Exercise 2-3, as you might expect, produces the following output:

```
This is line number: 0
This is line number: 1
This is line number: 2
This is line number: 3
This is line number: 4
```

Note the scope of the **lineno** variable. The variable is in scope for the current block and all blocks subordinate to the current one. Its scope, however, begins where the declaration appears. C++ statements that appear before the declaration cannot refer to the variable even though they might appear in the same block as the variable's declaration.

The Global Scope Resolution Operator

In C, if a local variable and a global variable have the same name, all references to that name while the local variable is in scope will refer to the local variable. Local variable names in C override global variable names. You must be aware of and program for this characteristic of C. If you want to refer to a global variable when a local one has the same name, you must change the name of one of the two.

C++ offers a different approach to this situation. You can tell the compiler that you want to refer to a global variable rather than the local one with the same name by using the **::** global scope resolution operator. The global scope resolution operator, which is coded as a prefix to the variable's name (for example, **::varname**), lets you explicitly reference a global variable from a scope where a local variable has the same name.

Exercise 2-4 is an example of how you use the scope resolution operator.

```
#include <iostream.h>

int amount = 123;        // a global variable

main()
{
    int amount = 456;    // a local variable

    cout << ::amount;    // display the global variable
    cout << amount;      // display the local variable
}
```

Exercise 2-4 — Global Scope Resolution Operator.

The exercise has two variables named **amount**. The first one is global and contains the value 123. The second **amount** variable is local to the **main** function.

The first **cout** statement displays 123, the contents of the global **amount** variable because that reference to the variable name uses the **::** global scope resolution operator. The second **cout** statement displays 456, the contents of the local **amount** variable because that reference to the variable name has no global scope resolution operator and defaults to the local variable in the traditional C fashion.

Exercise 2-4 displays the following output:

```
123456
```

`inline` **Functions**

You can tell the C++ compiler that a function is **inline**. This causes a new copy of it to be compiled in line each time it is called. The in-line nature of the individual copies eliminates the function-calling overhead of a traditional function. Obviously, you should use the **inline** function qualifier only when the function itself is small.

Exercise 2-5 uses the **inline** keyword to make a small and frequently used function into an **inline** function.

```
#include <iostream.h>
#include <stdlib.h>

inline void error_message(char *s)
{
    cout << '\a' << '\n' << s;
    exit(1);
}

main()
{
    error_message("You called?");
}
```

*Exercise 2-5 — An **in-line** Function.*

Exercise 2-5 sounds the computer's audible alarm and displays the message, "You called?" on the screen.

Observe that the exercise declares the **inline** function ahead of any calls to it. The *AT&T C++ Reference Manual* does not define where an **inline** function must be declared as such and under what conditions the compiler may choose to ignore the **inline** declaration except to say that the compiler may do so. Because of this ambiguity in the language specification, compiler builders have leeway in how they interpret the requirements. You could desire and declare an **inline** function (for performance reasons, perhaps) and have the compiler overrule you without saying so. To be safe, always declare **inline** functions ahead of all calls to them. If an **inline** function is to assume the appearance of an **extern** global function, that is, if it is to be called by code in several source files, put its declaration in a header file.

The `const` **Variable**

C++, like C, supports the **const** variable type qualifier. The **const** qualifier specifies that a variable is read-only, except during its one-time initialization. Nowhere other than through initialization can a program write a value into a **const** variable. C++ carries the

const idea one step further and treats such variables as if they were true constant expressions. Wherever you can use a constant expression, you can use a variable that has the **const** type qualifier. The ANSI X3J11 C Standards committee attempted to address this issue and define the **const** usage for the C language, but the result was mostly an ambiguous, although harmless, mess. C++ uses the **const** qualifier in a meaningful way.

Exercise 2-6 is an example of how you can use the **const** qualifier.

```
#include <iostream.h>

main()
{
    const int size = 5;
    char cs[size];

    cout << "The size of cs is " << sizeof cs;
}
```

Exercise 2-6 — The **const** *Variable Qualifier.*

Exercise 2-6 displays the following message.

```
The size of cs is 5
```

There are limitations to this usage. You cannot initialize the **const** variable with anything other than a constant expression; therefore you cannot use the syntax to derive dynamically dimensioned arrays. There are other ways to do that, and Chapter 3 will explain them.

enum **as a Type**

The **enum** in C++ is the same as **enum** in C with one exception: All declarations of instances of a C **enum** must include the **enum** keyword. A C++ **enum** becomes a data type when you define it; therefore, once defined, it is known by its identifier alone, the same as any other type, and declarations may use the identifier name alone.

Exercise 2-7 demonstrates how a C++ program can reference an **enum** data type by using the identifier without the **enum** qualifier.

```cpp
#include <iostream.h>

enum ignition_parts {
    distributor=1, cap, points, plug, condenser,
    coil, wires, done
};

main()
{
    ignition_parts ip;
    do    {
        cout << "\nEnter part number (1-7, 8 to quit): ";
        int pn;
        cin >> pn;
        ip = (ignition_parts) pn;
        switch ( ip )    {
            case distributor: cout << "Distributor";
                              break;
            case cap:         cout << "Distributor cap";
                              break;
            case points:      cout << "Ignition points";
                              break;
            case plug:        cout << "Spark plug";
                              break;
            case condenser:   cout << "Condenser";
                              break;
            case coil:        cout << "Ignition coil";
                              break;
            case wires:       cout << "Coil, plug wires";
                              break;
            case done:        break;
            default:          cout << "Unknown part number";
                              break;
        }
    } while (ip != done);
}
```

*Exercise 2-7 — **enum** as a Data Type.*

Exercise 2-7 displays these messages. You type the digits 1–7 and ∅, followed by the Enter key after each of the prompts.

```
Enter part number (1-7, Ø to quit): 1
Distributor
Enter part number (1-7, Ø to quit): 2
Distributor cap
Enter part number (1-7, Ø to quit): 3
Ignition points
Enter part number (1-7, Ø to quit): 4
Spark plug
Enter part number (1-7, Ø to quit): 5
Condenser
Enter part number (1-7, Ø to quit): 6
Ignition coil
Enter part number (1-7, Ø to quit): 7
Coil, plug wires
Enter part number (1-7, Ø to quit): Ø
```

This exercise translates a part number into its name. The **enum** associates the numbers 1 to 7 with identifiers that associate with the names of the parts. Observe that the declaration of the data item **ip** uses only the **enum** name, **ignition_parts**, and does not use the **enum** keyword itself. Because **ignition_parts** is a new data type, you do not need to further qualify it with the **enum** keyword.

> The program in Exercise 2-7 has some extra steps to accommodate Zortech C++. The data entry reads into the **pn** integer from **cin** rather than directly into the **ip** variable. The Zortech implementation of input/output streams does not allow you to read **cin** into an enumerated data type. Other C++ implementations allow that practice, which is correct C++. Zortech allows you to cast the receiving variable to an **int** (The first edition of this book did that to get around the problem.) Borland C++ does not complain and allows it. Other C++ implementations, particularly the CFRONT ports, do not allow the cast because it is incorrect to cast a receiving data type — an **lvalue** — even though the actual type and the cast are identical with respect to format and content.

continued...

…from previous page

> The **done** value within the **ignition_parts** type is set to the value 8 rather than **0**. Oddly, the Zortech **cin** object cannot read an integer that has a zero value. Other C++ implementations of **cin** work correctly with a zero value input.

Linkage-specifications

This next feature is not so much a C++ improvement to C as a way that the two languages can co-exist. It is discussed here because it will be used in later exercises.

A *linkage-specification* is the technique that C++ employs to make functions that were compiled by a C compiler accessible to a C++ program. There are differences in the way the two languages build external names, so if you are calling functions that were compiled by a C compiler, you must tell that fact to the C++ compiler.

The two languages use different linkage systems to support type-safe linkage, a feature that insures that calls to functions in separately compiled source modules match the definitions of the functions with respect to parameter types. The C++ compiler internally modifies each function's name with suffixes that identify the parameter types. Use of these (so-called) mangled names allows duplicate function names to exist across separately compiled source files, and allows the linker to properly resolve calls to the functions. The mangled names also transcend the use of prototypes to insure that the functions and their calls match. You cannot override the C++ type-checking simply by using different prototypes for the same function (as you can in C).

The C compiler does not mangle function names. Therefore, you must tell the C++ compiler when a function has been (or must be) compiled with C linkage conventions.

Exercise 2-8 shows how the linkage-specification tells the C++ compiler that the functions in *stdlib.h* were compiled by a C compiler.

```
#include <iostream.h>

extern "C"    {       // the linkage-specification
#include <stdlib.h>   // tells C++ that stdlib functions
}                     // were compiled with C

main()
{
    cout << rand();
}
```

Exercise 2-8 — Linkage-specifications.

Exercise 2-8 displays a single random number on the screen.

The **extern "C"** statement says that everything within the scope of the brace-surrounded block (<stdlib.h>) is compiled by a C compiler. If you do not use the braces, the linkage-specification deals only with the statement that immediately follows the C string.

Usually you will put the linkage-specification in the header file that contains the prototypes for the C programs. Language environments that support both languages often manage the translation for you by hiding the linkage specification in the standard header files for the C functions. So, for the most part, you can be unaware of the difference between C functions and C++ functions. The exercises in this book assume that such files as *stdlib.h* and *string.h* include the appropriate linkage-specification.

There are times, however, when you will need to use linkage-specifications outside the realm of standard C header files. If you have a large library of custom C functions to include in your C++ system, and you do not want to take the time and trouble to port them to C++ (perhaps you do not have the source code), then you must use a linkage-specification. If, within a C linkage-specification, you have some C++ prototypes, you can code a nested C++ linkage-specification.

Occasionally you will need to tell the C++ compiler to compile a function with C linkages. You would do this if the function was to be called from a function that was itself compiled with C linkages (usually a function from your C library).

Exercise 2-9 is an example of a C++ program that calls a function that is compiled with a C compiler and has C linkages. The C++ program includes a function that will be called from the C program and must be compiled with C linkages.

```cpp
#include <iostream.h>

// --------- array of string pointers to be sorted
static const char *brothers[] = {
    "Frederick William",
    "Joseph Jensen",
    "Harry Alan",
    "Walter Ellsworth",
    "Julian Paul"
};

// ------ prototype of functions compiled in C
extern "C" void SortCharArray(const char **);

// ------ C++ function to be called from the C program
extern "C"    {
  int SizeArray(void)
  {
      return sizeof brothers / sizeof (char*);
  }
}

main()
{
    // --------- sort the pointers
    SortCharArray(brothers);
    // --------- display the brothers in sorted order
    int size = SizeArray();
    for (int i = 0; i < size; i++)
        cout << '\n' << brothers[i];
}
```

Exercise 2-9a — The C++ Source.

Exercise 2-9a displays these messages.

```
Frederick William
Harry Alan
Joseph Jensen
Julian Paul
Walter Ellsworth
```

```
/* C program for linkage-specifications */
/*
 * A C program compiled with a C compiler to demonstrate
 * C linkage to a C++ program
 */

#include <string.h>
#include <stdlib.h>

static int comp(const void *a, const void *b);
int SizeArray(void); /* The C++ function */

void SortCharArray(const char **List)
{
    qsort(List, SizeArray(), sizeof(char *), comp);
}

/* ----- the compare function for qsort ---- */
static int comp(const void *a, const void *b)
{
    return strcmp(*(char **)a, *(char **)b);
}
```

Exercise 2-9b — The C Source.

Exercise 2-9 consists of two source files, a C++ program (2-9a) and a C function (2-9b). The C function, will sort an array of character pointers but does not know the length of the array. It must, therefore, call a function — whose name must be **SizeArray** and which must be provided by the caller — to determine the length of the array. The C++ program declares two C linkages — one for the **SortCharArray** C function that the C++ program calls, and one for its own **SizeArray** function that the C function calls.

Without the linkage-specifications, the C++ compiler will mangle the names of the C++ function and the C++ program's call to the C function. The linker will not be able to resolve the C++ program's call to the **SortCharArray** C function or the C function's call to the **SizeArray** C++ function.

> In the real world, you would take other measures to give the length of the array to the C function. You could **NULL**-terminate the array, and the C function could determine the array length on its own. You could pass the length of the array as an argument to the C function. You could pass the address of a function in the C++ program, which would then not need to be compiled with C linkages (unless you are using Zortech C++). Perhaps you are not in control of the C program, not having its source code, and you are stuck with whatever conventions the C programmer used. Perhaps the C function is already so widely used that you cannot change it.

Languages other than C and C++ can be supported by linkage-specifications, and their string values will depend on the whims of the compiler builders.

Anonymous unions

A C++ program can define an unnamed **union** anywhere it can have a variable. You might use this feature to save space, or you might use it to intentionally redefine a variable.

Exercise 2-10 illustrates the use of the anonymous **union**.

```
#include <iostream.h>

main()
{
    union    {
        int quantity_todate;
        int quantity_balance;
    };

    cout << "Enter quantity to date: ";
    cin >> quantity_todate;

    cout << "Enter quantity sold: ";
    int quantity_sold;
    cin >> quantity_sold;

    quantity_todate -= quantity_sold;
    cout << "Quantity balance = " << quantity_balance;
}
```

Exercise 2-10 — Anonymous **unions**.

The program in Exercise 2-10 allows the two variables **quantity_todate** and **quantity_balance** to share the same space. After it subtracts **quantity_sold** from **quantity_todate**, **quantity_balance** contains the following result as well:

```
Enter quantity to date: 100
Enter quantity sold: 75
Quantity balance = 25
```

This feature eliminates a lot of **union** name prefixes in places where the only purpose for the **union** name is to support the **union**.

You must declare a global anonymous **union** as static.

Unnamed Function Parameters

You can declare a C function that has one or more parameters that the function does not use. This circumstance occurs when you write several functions that are called through a generic function pointer. Some of the functions do not use all of the parameters. Following is an example of such a function.

```
func(int x, int y)
{
    return x * 2;
}
```

Although this usage is correct and common, most C and C++ compilers will complain that you failed to use the parameter named **y**. C++, however, allows you to declare functions with unnamed parameters to indicate to the compiler that the parameter exists, the caller will pass an argument for the parameter, but the called function will not use it. Following is the C++ function coded with an unnamed second parameter.

```
func(int x, int)
{
    return x * 2;
}
```

Constructors for Intrinsic Data Types

C++ Version 2.1 allows you to initialize the intrinsic data types, such as **int**, **long**, **double**, etc., by using the notation of a class constructor. You will learn about class constructors in Chapter 7. The following statements are valid initialized variable declarations in C++ Version 2.1.

```
int qty(123);
double spec(5.378);
```

The two statements just shown have the same effect as these traditional C declaration initialization statements.

```
int qty = 123;
double spec = 5.378;
```

Summary

What you have learned so far have been ways that C++ improves the C language. Each subsequent chapter is more of the same, but the improvements that follow are what set C++ apart as its own language rather than as just an improved C. You can use these new features in ways unrelated to the object-oriented paradigm, or you can totally immerse yourself in the paradigm and use C++ as your object-oriented development environment.

Chapter 3

The C++ Free Store

A s a C programmer, you use the **malloc** and **free** family of functions to allocate and manage memory from the system heap. C++ offers a better way through the use of the **new** and **delete** operators of the C++ free store. These operators work to associate the allocation of memory with the way you use it. In the C++ lexicon, free store means heap, and **new** and **delete** are similar to **malloc** and **free**.

There is a great deal to know about the free store and its behavior, and there are lessons to be learned by studying this better approach. The fledgling C++ programmer should not minimize the importance of a clear understanding of this aspect of the language.

The new and delete Operators

The **new** operator, when used with the name of a pointer to a data type, structure, or array, allocates memory for the item and assigns the address of that memory to the pointer.

The **delete** operator returns the memory owned by the variable to the free store. Although **new** and **delete** work the same on all data types, their use is best understood at first when used with a structure.

Exercise 3-1 is your first use of the **new** and **delete** operators.

```
#include <iostream.h>

struct Date {          // a date structure
    int month;
    int day;
    int year;
};

main()
{
    Date *birthday = new Date;    // get memory for a date
    birthday->month = 6;          // assign a value to the date
    birthday->day = 24;
    birthday->year = 1940;
    cout << "I was born on "      // display the date
        << birthday->month << '/'
        << birthday->day   << '/'
        << birthday->year;
    delete birthday;              // return memory to the free store
}
```

*Exercise 3-1 — The C++ Free Store: The **new** and **delete** Operators.*

Exercise 3-1 displays this message:

`I was born on 6/24/1940`

This exercise has a structure that defines a date. The program uses the **new** operator to get some memory for an instance of the structure. Then it initializes the new structure with a date. After displaying the contents of the structure, the program disposes of it by using the **delete** operator.

> Note that the declaration of the **birthday** pointer does not include the **struct** keyword. This omission would appear to the C programmer to be an error. However, it is not an error, but another of the improvements in C++. You will learn more about this in Chapter 5.

Allocating a Fixed-dimension Array

Many of the advantages of **new** and **delete** over the C functions **malloc** and **free** were not illustrated in Exercise 3-1. They appear to be the same. However, **new** and **delete** provide a more readable syntax for memory allocation.

Exercise 3-2 shows how you can use **new** and **delete** to acquire and then dispose of memory for an array.

```
#include <iostream.h>

main()
{
    int *birthday = new int[3];    // get memory for a date array
    birthday[0] = 6;               // assign a value to the date
    birthday[1] = 24;
    birthday[2] = 1940;
    cout << "I was born on "       // display the date
         << birthday[0] << '/'
         << birthday[1] << '/'
         << birthday[2];
    delete birthday;    // return memory to the free store
}
```

*Exercise 3-2 — The C++ Free Store: **new** and **delete** with an Array.*

Exercise 3-2 displays the same message as Exercise 3-1.

Allocating Dynamic Arrays

The fact that the **new** operator recognizes a data type with an array dimension was shown in Exercise 3-2. The dimension in the exercise is a constant 3, representing the number of integers in the date. You can, however, supply a variable dimension, and the **new** operator allocates the correct amount of memory.

Exercise 3-3 shows the use of a variably dimensioned array as allocated by the new operator.

```
#include <iostream.h>
#include <stdlib.h>

main()
{
    cout << "Enter the array size: ";
    int size;
    cin >> size;                     // get the array size
    int *array = new int[size];      // allocate an array
    for (int i = 0; i < size; i++)   // load the array
        array[i] = rand();           // with random numbers
    for (i = 0; i < size; i++)       // display the array
        cout << '\n' << array[i];
    delete array; // return the array to the free store
}
```

Exercise 3-3 — The C++ Free Store: **new** *with a Dynamic Array.*

In this exercise, type in the size of the array when you run the program. The **new** operator uses the value that you enter to establish the size of memory to be allocated and later as the subscript for the delete operator. The program then builds the array by using the **new** operator, fills it with random numbers, displays each of the elements in the array, and deletes the array by using the **delete** operator.

Exercise 3-3 displays the following messages: (The 5 is the number you would enter. The five other numbers are random numbers generated by the **rand**() function.)

```
Enter the array size: 5
346
130
10982
1090
11656
```

Exercise 3-4 offers another variation on the dynamically dimensioned array through the **new** operator, in this case the use of a function call to compute the dimension. The object of this program is to read a number of variable-length strings from the user, sort them, and display them in a left-justified column.

> Observe the use of the C linkage-specification to describe the **comp** function. The Zortech 2.1 compiler requires the linkage-specification even though you are passing the address of a C++ function and not asking the C function to call a specifically named C++ function. Other C++ implementations do not require the linkage specification in this context.

```
#include <iostream.h>
#include <stdlib.h>
#include <string.h>

// ---------- compare function to sort array of pointers
extern "C"     {
  int comp(const void *a, const void *b)
  {
      return strcmp(*(char **)a, *(char **)b);
  }
}


main()
{
    cout << "How many names at most? ";
    int maxnames;
    cin >> maxnames;
    char **names = new char *[maxnames];
    char *name = new char[80];
    for (int namect = 0; namect < maxnames; namect++)     {
        cout << "Enter a name ('end' if done before "
                << maxnames << " names): ";
        cin >> name;
        if (strcmp(name, "end") == 0)
            break;
        names[namect] = new char[strlen(name)+1];
        strcpy(names[namect], name);
    }
    qsort(names, namect, sizeof(char *), comp);
    for (int i = 0; i < namect; i++)
        cout << names[i] << '\n';
    for (i = 0; i < namect; i++)
        delete names[i];
    delete name;
    delete names;
}
```

Exercise 3-4 — The C++ Free Store: More Dynamic Array Allocation.

The program in Exercise 3-4 begins by asking you to enter the maximum number of names. From the value you enter, the program allocates an array of character pointers named **names**. Then you begin entering names. For each name, the program allocates a new array with its address in the **names** array. When you enter the name "end" or after you have entered as many names as you said you would, the program displays all of them.

Exercise 3-4 displays these messages: (The 6 is the number of names you intend to enter. The Bill, Sam, Paul, Spoof, Jim, and Chick entries are the names you could enter. The sorted list of the same names follows the entries.)

```
How many names at most? 6
Enter a name ('end' if done before 6 names): Bill
Enter a name ('end' if done before 6 names): Sam
Enter a name ('end' if done before 6 names): Paul
Enter a name ('end' if done before 6 names): Spoof
Enter a name ('end' if done before 6 names): Jim
Enter a name ('end' if done before 6 names): Chick
Bill
Chick
Jim
Paul
Sam
Spoof
```

When the Store is Exhausted

So far these exercises have not considered the question of what to do if the free store is out of memory when you use the **new** operator. Instead, they just assume that the store will never be exhausted. Clearly, this is not a real-world approach. The C **malloc** function returns a NULL pointer under that condition, and C programs that call **malloc** usually test for the NULL return and do something meaningful about it.

The _new_handler Function Pointer

You could take the same approach with C++ by simply testing each use of the **new** operator for a NULL return; **new** returns a NULL pointer if there is no memory to allocate. There is a better way, however. C++ includes a global function pointer named **_new_handler**. Normally, that pointer is NULL, and when new runs out of memory, new returns NULL. But if the **_new_handler** function pointer contains a non-NULL value, **new** assumes that the value is the address to call when memory is exhausted.

The `set_new_handler` Function

C++ includes a function named **set_new_handler** that lets you set the **_new_handler** function pointer.

Exhausting the Free Store

If the **new** operator finds itself out of free-store space, it calls the function pointed to by **_new_handler**.

Exercise 3-5 illustrates a **_new_handler** function that terminates the program when the free store is gone.

```
#include <iostream.h>
#include <stdlib.h>
#include <new.h>

static void all_gone()
{
    cerr << "\n\aThe free store is empty\n";
    exit(1);
}

main()
{
    set_new_handler(all_gone);
    long total = 0;
    while (1)   {
        char *gobble = new char[10000];
        total += 10000;
        cout << "Got 10000 for a total of " << total << '\n';
    }
}
```

3-5 — Free Store Exhaustion and the **_new_handler** *Function.*

This exercise goes into a loop consuming free store and displaying messages about it. When the store is empty, the **new** operator turns things over to the **all_gone** function, which sends an error message to **cerr** and exits.

Exercise 3-5 would display the following messages:

```
Got 10000 for a total of 10000
Got 10000 for a total of 20000
Got 10000 for a total of 30000
Got 10000 for a total of 40000
Got 10000 for a total of 50000
Got 10000 for a total of 60000
The free store is empty
```

> The TopSpeed C++ compiler uses the .HPP extension for most of its C++ header files. It will substitute IOSTREAM.HPP when you code IOSTREAM.H, but it does not do that for some of the other header files. Therefore, if you are using TopSpeed C++, the #include <new.h> preprocessing directive must be changed to #include <new.hpp>.

Going for More Store

If your **_new_handler** function returns, the **new** operator tries again to allocate the required memory. This opens the door for a programmer to try to do something about free-store exhaustion. What you do would depend on how your free store works. The default **new** and **delete** operators take their memory from the heap. Heap management is an implementation-dependent operation, and anything you might do to increase the memory available to the default **new** operator would not be portable to other systems, perhaps not even to other C++ compilers on the same system.

Rolling Your Own `new` **and** `delete` Operators

The default **new** and **delete** operators are general-purpose enough to suffice for most programming situations. There could be times, however, when your program wants more control over what happens when the **new** operator executes. For example, the default **new** operator does not initialize the memory that is allocated. Perhaps you want to set all the space to zeros. To do this, you build your own **new** operator.

> You are about to learn how to install your own dynamic memory manager into your C++ environment. This ability implies a certain amount of responsibility. Overloading the global **new** and **delete** operators puts your functions in the position of allocating and freeing dynamic memory for all global uses of the free store, including **new** and **delete** calls from within the compiler's library functions and startup code. Although C++ provides this powerful overloading facility, most programmers do not find it necessary to replace the global **new** and **delete** functions provided by the compiler.

Exercise 3-6 is an example of a custom-built **new** operator that initializes memory to zeros before returning.

```
#include <iostream.h>
#include <stdlib.h>
#include <stddef.h>

// ------------- overloaded new operator
void *operator new(size_t size)
{
    void *rtn = calloc(1, size);
    return rtn;
}

// ----------- overloaded delete operator
void operator delete(void *type)
{
    free(type);
}

main()
{
    // ------ allocate a zero-filled array
    int *ip = new int[10];
    // ------ display the array
    for (int i = 0; i < 10; i++)
        cout << ' ' << ip[i];
    // ----- release the memory
    delete ip;
}
```

*Exercise 3-6 — Home-brew **new** and **delete**.*

Exercise 3-6 displays this message of zero values.

0 0 0 0 0 0 0 0 0 0

This exercise is an early look at operator overloading, a powerful feature of C++. The **new** and **delete** keywords are implemented in C++ as operators, and you can redefine their meaning within the context of how they are called by writing **operator** functions that replace them. Chapter 8 is dedicated to the subject of overloaded operators within the context of the new C++ classes you might develop.

The overloaded **new** operator in Exercise 3-6 uses the standard C **calloc** function to get memory. That function allocates memory and sets it to zero, so your work is done for you.

Exercise 3-7 shows how you can build and use an overloaded **new** operator with additional parameters. For this exercise, the **new** operator will fill memory with a character selected by your use of the operator.

```
#include <iostream.h>
#include <stdlib.h>
#include <string.h>
#include <stddef.h>

// ------------ overloaded new operator
void *operator new(size_t size, int filler)
{
    void *rtn;
    if ((rtn = malloc(size)) != NULL)
        memset(rtn, filler, size);
    return rtn;
}

// ----------- overloaded delete operator
void operator delete(void *type)
{
    free(type);
}

main()
{
    // ------ allocate an asterisk-filled array
    char *cp = new ('*') char[10];
    // ------ display the array
    for (int i = 0; i < 10; i++)
        cout << ' ' << cp[i];
    // ----- release the memory
    delete cp;
}
```

*Exercise 3-7 — Home-brew **new** and **delete** with Character Fill.*

This exercise shows you how to add parameters to the **new** operator. The first parameter must be an integer type and, in the default **new**, is the *only* parameter. But you can provide additional parameters as shown in Exercise 3-7. The use of the **new** operator in that exercise shows you how to pass parameters to the overloaded **new**.

None of these overloaded **new** operators acknowledges the role of the **_new_handler** function pointer. It is with an overloaded **new** operator that you can take advantage of this feature. Because you supply the memory allocator, you are in the best position to develop the strategy for dealing with memory exhaustion.

Exercise 3-8 shows how you would connect your **new** operator to your **_new_handler** function, without actually solving the problem of memory exhaustion.

```
#include <iostream.h>
#include <stdlib.h>
#include <string.h>
#include <stddef.h>

static void all_gone()
{
    cerr << "\n\aThe free store is empty\n";
    exit(1);
}

extern void (*_new_handler)();

// ------------- overloaded new operator
static void *operator new(size_t size)
{
    void *rtn;
    while((rtn = malloc(size)) == NULL)
        if (_new_handler != NULL)
            (*_new_handler)();
        else
            break;
    memset(rtn, '\0', size);
    return rtn;
}

// ----------- overloaded delete operator
```

Exercise 3-8 continued...

...from previous page

```
void operator delete(void *type)
{
    free(type);
}

main()
{
    _new_handler = all_gone;
    // ----- now get more than exists
    char *ip1 = new char[40000];
    char *ip2 = new char[40000];
}
```

Exercise 3-8 — Home-brew **new** *and* **delete** *with a* **_new_handler***.*

Exercise 3-8 sounds the audible alarm and displays this message:

```
The free store is empty
```

> Some C++ 2.1 compilers — TopSpeed C++, for example — do not define an external **_new_handler** function pointer. This pointer is not defined in the current AT&T C++ 2.1 specification, although it was a part of 2.0. Exercise 3-8 will not run with compilers that do not have a global external **new_handler** function pointer.

You can use your custom **new** operator and the default **new** operator in the same program if the custom **new** has different parameter types than the default one.

Exercise 3-9 illustrates how the compiler selects the correct **new** operator function to call based on the types of the parameters in the use of the **new** operator.

```
#include <iostream.h>
#include <stdlib.h>
#include <string.h>
#include <stddef.h>

// ------------- overloaded new operator
static void *operator new(size_t size, int filler)
{
    cout << "\nRunning new\n";
    void *rtn = malloc(size);
    if (rtn != NULL)
        memset(rtn, filler, size);
    return rtn;
}

// ----------- overloaded delete operator
void operator delete(void *type)
{
    cout << "\nDeleting";
    free(type);
}

main()
{
    // ------ allocate an array with the custom new
    char *cp = new ('*') char[10];
    // ---- use the default new for this allocation
    int *ip = new int[10];
    // ---- release the memory (both use our delete)
    delete ip;
    delete cp;
}
```

Exercise 3-9 — Home-brew **new** *and* **delete** *with Delete Contention.*

There is an anomaly to this usage, however. Because you can overload the delete operator only with its originally defined **void *** parameter, your custom **delete** will execute for all your uses of **delete**. This is *not* true when you build custom **new** and **delete** operators for C++ classes. (You are not at that point yet; wait until Chapter 7.)

Exercise 3-9 displays messages on the console each time the **new** and **delete** operators execute. The following output is what the exercise displays:

```
Running new
Deleting
Deleting
```

As you can see, the custom **new** executes once, but the custom **delete** executes twice. The only way you can be sure that this will work is to know that in your C++ environment, the default **delete** calls the C **free** function, and that might not always be the case. As a rule, you should overload the **new** and **delete** operators only in the context where you will use the overloaded versions exclusively.

Programs compiled with Borland C++ always use the **delete** operator twice when the program exits. The example output given above will show two extra "Deleting" messages. Apparently the start-up and shut-down procedures of a Borland C++ program use the free store. If you overload the global **delete** operator, you must be sure to do so in a manner that will be consistent with Borland's use of it, which means that you must use the heap's **free** function and little else.

Summary

This chapter dealt with the basics of the C++ free store and the **new** and **delete** operators. You will learn more about these aspects of C++ in later chapters where their advanced features contribute to C++ class construction.

During your excursion into **new** and **delete**, you received an introduction to overloaded operators. Overloading is one of the more powerful facilities in C++. You can overload operators, and you can overload functions. Chapter 4 deals with the overloading of functions.

Chapter 4

Overloaded Functions

You can reuse a function name in a C program if you want the new function to replace the old one for as long as the new one is in scope. The two functions cannot, however, share the same scope. If you want to have two similar C functions with slightly different operations on different parameter types, you must write two different C functions. The standard C **strcpy** and **strncpy** functions are examples.

C++ has a better way. It allows you to reuse a function name in the same scope, but with different parameter types. Both versions of the function are then available at the same time. This feature is called **function overloading** and is the subject of this chapter. Function overloading is when you redefine a function in a way that makes multiple versions of the same function name available to the same program.

Overloading for Different Operations

Sometimes you want to overload a function because it performs a generic task, but there are different permutations of what it does. The standard C **strcpy** and **strncpy** functions are examples. Both functions copy strings, but they do so in slightly different ways. The **strcpy** function simply copies a string from the source to the destination. The **strncpy** function copies a string, but stops copying when the source string terminates or after it copies a specified number of characters. These functions are likely candidates to be members of an overloaded function family.

Exercise 4-1 replaces the standard C **strcpy** and **strncpy** functions with the single function name, **string_copy**.

```
#include <iostream.h>

void string_copy(char *dest, const char *src)
{
    while((*dest++ = *src++) != '\0')
        ;
}

void string_copy(char *dest, const char *src, int len)
{
    while (len && (*dest++ = *src++) != '\0')
        -len;
    while (len-)
        *dest++ = '\0';
}

static char misspiggie[20], kermit[20];

main()
{
    string_copy(misspiggie, "Miss Piggie");
    string_copy(kermit,
        "Kermit the file transfer protocol", 6);
    cout << kermit << " and " << misspiggie;
}
```

Exercise 4-1 — Overloading Functions for Different Operations.

Exercise 4-1 displays this message.

```
Kermit and Miss Piggie
```

There are two functions named **string_copy** in this program. What sets them apart is their different parameter lists. The first of the two **string_copy** functions has destination and source character pointers as parameters. The second function has the pointers and an integer length as well. The C++ compiler recognizes that these are two distinct functions by virtue of these differences in their parameter lists.

Overloading for Different Formats

How you might overload a function to get a different algorithm on similar data was demonstrated in exercise 4-1. Another reason to overload a function is to get the same result from data values that can be represented in different formats. Standard C has different ways of representing the date and time. You will find more ways in Unix, and still others in MS-DOS.

Exercise 4-2 shows how you can send two of the standard C formats to the overloaded **display_time** function.

```
#include <iostream.h>
#include <time.h>

void display_time(const struct tm *tim)
{
    cout << "1. It is now " << asctime(tim);
}

void display_time(time_t *tim)
{
    cout << "2. It is now " << ctime(tim);
}

main()
{
    time_t tim = time((time_t *)NULL);
    struct tm *ltim = localtime(&tim);

    display_time(ltim);
    display_time(&tim);
}
```

Exercise 4-2 — Overloaded Functions for Different Data Formats.

The exercise uses the standard C data formats **time_t** and **struct tm**. It gets the value of the current date and time into them with the **time** and **localtime** functions. Then it calls its own overloaded **display_time** function once for each of the formats.

Exercise 4-2 displays the following results:

```
1. It is now Wed May 15 12:05:20 1991
2. It is now Wed May 15 12:05:20 1991
```

Dates and times are good ways to experiment with overloaded functions. There are many ways to internally represent them, many ways that different systems report them to a program, and many ways to display them. In addition to all these formats, there are many common date and time algorithms. A comprehensive date and time package would be a solid addition to any programmer's tool collection.

Summary

Function overloading is one of the facets of C++ that supports the object-oriented programming view of things. However, as this chapter shows, you can use its features in your traditional programming environment to design and develop programs that are more readable.

Chapter 5

C++ Structures

C++ structures are similar to C structures, but they can have more features. This chapter describes the characteristics of the C++ structure that makes it unique from C, and it does so in a way that brings the programmer closer to the object-oriented paradigm.

Structures as Data Types

When you define a structure in C++, you have defined a new data type and added it to the language. In C, every declaration of an instance of a defined structure must include the **struct** keyword, as in the following example:

```
/* --- defining a C structure --- */
struct Date {int month,day,year;};
/* --- declaring a C structure --- */
struct Date today;
```

In C++, a structure is its own data type and can be known by its own name without requiring the **struct** keyword.

Exercise 5-1 shows the various ways you can use a structure's name in C++.

```
#include <iostream.h>

// ------ structure = data type
struct Date {
    int month;
    int day;
    int year;
};

static void display(Date);              // a date parameter

main()
{
    static Date birthday = {10,12,1962}; // a date
    Date dates[10];                      // an array of dates
    Date *dp = dates;                    // a pointer to a date

    for (int i = 0; i < 10; i++)    {
        *(dp + i) = birthday;
        dates[i].year += i;
        cout << "\nOn ";
        display(dates[i]);
        cout << " Sharon was ";
        if (i > 0)
            cout << i;
        else
            cout << "born";
    }
}

static void display(Date dt)
{
    static char *mon[] = {
        "January","February","March","April","May","June",
        "July","August","September","October","November",
        "December"};
    cout << mon[dt.month-1] << ' ' << dt.day << ", "
        << dt.year;
}
```

Exercise 5-1 — The Structure as a Data Type.

The exercise defines a **Date** structure with a member for each of the elements **day**, **month**, and **year**. The **main** function contains an instance of the structure, an array of the structure, a pointer to the structure, and a prototype of a function that accepts the structure as a parameter. Yet the keyword **struct** does not appear in any of these objects because **Date** became a data type when the date structure was defined.

Exercise 5-1 displays the following messages:

```
On October 12, 1962 Sharon was born
On October 12, 1963 Sharon was 1
On October 12, 1964 Sharon was 2
On October 12, 1965 Sharon was 3
On October 12, 1966 Sharon was 4
On October 12, 1967 Sharon was 5
On October 12, 1968 Sharon was 6
On October 12, 1969 Sharon was 7
On October 12, 1970 Sharon was 8
On October 12, 1971 Sharon was 9
```

Structures with Functions

A structure is an aggregate of data types. Grouping the different members together forms a record of sorts with different fields. The structure can contain integers, floats, arrays, pointers, typedefs, unions, and other data types. In other words, any valid data type can be a member of a structure. This convention is consistent with the C definition of a structure. C++ adds another type of member to the structure. In C++, structures can include functions.

A Glimpse at Object-Oriented Programming

Take a moment to consider the implications of this new ability. By adding functions to structures, you add the ability for a structure to include algorithms that are bound to, and work with, the other structure members. You closely associate the algorithms with the data they process; this is one of the fundamental concepts of the object-oriented program.

Adding Functions to Structures

Exercise 5-2 is a program that adds a function to the **Date** structure in exercise 5-1. The function's name is **display**, and its purpose will be to display the contents of an instance of the **Date** structure.

```
#include <iostream.h>

// ------  structure with a function
struct Date {
    int month, day, year;
    void display(void);      // a function to display the date
};

void Date::display()
{
    static char *mon[] = {
        "January","February","March","April","May","June",
        "July","August","September","October","November",
        "December"};
    cout << mon[month-1] << ' ' << day << ", " << year;
}

main()
{
    static Date birthday = {4, 6, 1961};
    cout << "Alan's date of birth was ";
    birthday.display();
}
```

Exercise 5-2 — Structures with Functions.

This exercise codes the **display** function's declaration as **Date::display**. This notation tells the C++ compiler that the **display** function exists to support instances of the **Date** structure. In fact, the only way to call this **display** function is as a member of a declared **Date**.

The **main** function declares a **Date** named **birthday** and initializes it with a value. Then the **main** function calls the **Date::display** function by identifying it as a member of the **birthday** structure using the following notation:

```
birthday.display();
```

The **Date::display** function displays the following date format:

```
Alan's date of birth was April 6, 1961
```

The **Date::display** function can reference members of the structure with which it is associated directly without naming an instance of the structure, because it is a member of the structure.

Multiple Instances of the Same Structure

As you might expect, you can declare more than one instance of the same structure, and the member function will associate itself with the data in the particular structure for which you call it.

Exercise 5-3 uses the **Date** structure in two places.

```
#include <iostream.h>

// ------  structure with a function
struct Date {
    int month, day, year;
    void display(void);    // a function to display the date
};

void Date::display()
{
    static char *mon[] = {
        "January","February","March","April","May","June",
        "July","August","September","October","November",
        "December"};
    cout << mon[month-1] << ' ' << day << ", " << year;
}

main()
{
    static Date alans_birthday = {4, 6, 1961};
    cout << "\nAlan's date of birth was ";
    alans_birthday.display();

    static Date wendys_birthday = {4, 28, 1965};
    cout << "\nWendy's date of birth was ";
    wendys_birthday.display();
}
```

Exercise 5-3 — Multiple Instances of a Structure with a Function.

The program declares two **Date** structures and uses the **display** function to display the following messages:

```
Alan's date of birth was April 6, 1961
Wendy's date of birth was April 28, 1965
```

Overloaded Stucture Functions

You can have different structure definitions that use the same function name. This is another form of function overloading that you learned in Chapter 4.

Exercise 5-4 is an example of two structures that each use a function named **display**.

```cpp
#include <iostream.h>
#include <stdio.h>
#include <time.h>

// ------  date structure with a function
struct Date {
    int month, day, year;
    void display(void);        // a function to display the date
};

void Date::display()
{
    static char *mon[] = {
        "January","February","March","April","May","June",
        "July","August","September","October","November",
        "December"};
    cout << mon[month] << ' ' << day << ", " << year;
}

// ------  time structure with a function
struct Time {
    int hour, minute, second;
```

Exercise 5-4 continued...

…from previous page

```
    void display(void);    // a function to display the clock
};

void Time::display()
{
    char tmsg[15];
    sprintf(tmsg, "%d:%02d:%02d %s",
        (hour > 12 ? hour - 12 : (hour == 0 ? 12 : hour)),
        minute, second,
        hour < 12 ? "am" : "pm");
    cout << tmsg;
}

main()
{
    // -------- get the current time from the OS
    time_t curtime = time((time_t *)NULL);
    struct tm tim = *localtime(&curtime);
    // --------- clock and date structures
    Time now;
    Date today;
    // --------- initialize the structures
    now.hour = tim.tm_hour;
    now.minute = tim.tm_min;
    now.second = tim.tm_sec;
    today.month = tim.tm_mon;
    today.day = tim.tm_mday;
    today.year = tim.tm_year+1900;
    // ---------- display the date and time
    cout << "At the tone it will be ";
    now.display();
    cout << " on ";
    today.display();
    cout << '\a';
}
```

Exercise 5-4 — Two Structures with the Same Function Name.

The program in exercise 5-4 has a **Date** structure and a **Time** structure. Both structures have functions named **display**. The **display** function that is associated with the **Date** structure displays the date; the **display** function that is associated with the **Time** function displays the time.

Exercise 5-4 sounds the audible alarm and displays the following message.

```
At the tone it will be 6:19:12 pm on May 3, 1991
```

The date and time will be the current ones.

Structure Access Specifiers

By default, the members of a structure are visible to all the functions that are within the scope of the structure object. You can limit this access with three "access specifiers" in the structure's definition. The **Date** structure in the earlier exercises might be modified with the **private** and **public** access specifiers as shown here.

```
struct Date {
private:
    int month, day, year;
public:
    void display(void);
};
```

All members following the **private** access specifier are accessible only to the member functions within the structure definition. All members following the **public** access specifier are accessible to any function that is within the scope of the structure. If you omit the access specifiers, everything is public. You can use an access specifier more than once in the same structure definition.

The **protected** access specifier is the same as the **private** access specifier unless the structure is a part of a class hierarchy, a subject that Chapter 9 addresses.

When you define a structure with the **private** and **protected** access specifiers, the structure begins to take on the properties of a class, and you should define it as such. You cannot, for example, initialize the structure shown above with a brace-separated list of integers because the data members are private to the class's member functions and are not visible to the rest of the program. You would need to define a "constructor" function, and perhaps a "destructor" function, to handle the structure's initialization when it comes into scope and destruction when it goes out of scope. These subjects take on meaning when you learn about C++ classes in Chapter 7.

Unions

C++ **unions** are similar to C **unions** in that the data members share the same memory, and only one of the members can contain a value at any one time. (You learned about C++ anonymous **unions** in Chapter 2.) C++ **unions** share some of the enhancements that C++ structures have. A **union** can have function members but it cannot be a part of a class hierarchy the way structures can. You will learn about classes in Chapter 7 and class hierarchies in Chapter 9. A **union** can have constructor and destructor functions (see Chapter 7), but it cannot have any virtual functions (see Chapter 9).

In C++ version 2.1, **unions** can have private and public members. You will learn more about the **private** and **public** access specifiers in Chapter 7.

Summary

This chapter has moved you closer to object-oriented programming. Structures that become data types and that have functions associated with them resemble closely the C++ class, which is the basic unit of the object-oriented paradigm. Chapter 6 discusses the C++ reference, a way to avoid the sometimes confusing world of the C pointer.

Chapter 6

References

T his chapter is about the C++ reference. The reference is a means for assigning, sending, and returning complex data structures, without the overhead usually associated with the physical memory transfers of those operations. It is also a way to remove the clutter that often accompanies pointer de-referencing in your code. And, as you will see, it has other advantages (as well as a few pitfalls).

If you are like most C programmers, the pointer gave you the most trouble when you first learned C. Veteran C programmers can still get bogged down trying to comprehend some of the complex operations that C pointers and pointers-to-pointers permit. The C++ reference variable can give you some of the same kind of trouble until you understand it, and it has some of its own wrinkles as well. Its syntax and usage, however, prevent many of the pointer pitfalls that trap C programmers.

The reference is one of the least-understood parts of C++ and one of the hardest to learn. The better you understand C pointers, the harder it seems to be to grasp exactly what references do.

The following is a list of things to remember when you deal with references. You will learn about each of these items in the paragraphs and exercises in this chapter.

- A reference is an alias for an actual variable.

- A reference must be initialized and cannot be changed.

- References can create hidden anonymous objects.

- References work best with user-defined data types.

- References are best used as function parameters.

- A function can return a reference.

- You can pass references to functions

- You can return references from functions

- You *cannot* do these things with references:

   - point to them

   - take the address of one

   - compare them

   - assign to them

   - do arithmetic to them

   - modify them

The Reference is an Alias

A C++ reference is an alias for another variable. When you declare a reference variable, you must give it a value which you may not change for the life of the reference. The **&** operator identifies a reference variable as in the following example:

```
int actualint;
int& otherint = actualint;
```

With these statements, you have declared an integer named **actualint** and you have told the compiler that **actualint** has another name, **otherint**. Now all references to either name have the same result.

Exercise 6-1 illustrates how a reference and the data item it refers to appear to be one and the same.

```
#include <iostream.h>

main()
{
    int actualint = 123;
    int& otherint = actualint;

    cout << '\n' << actualint;
    cout << '\n' << otherint;
    otherint++;
    cout << '\n' << actualint;
    cout << '\n' << otherint;
    actualint++;
    cout << '\n' << actualint;
    cout << '\n' << otherint;
}
```

Exercise 6-1 — The Reference.

The exercise shows that operations on **otherint** act upon **actualint**. Exercise 6-1 displays the following output, and it shows that whatever you do to **otherint**, you do to **actualint**, and vice versa:

```
123
123
124
124
125
125
```

The alias metaphor is an almost perfect one. A reference is neither a copy of nor a pointer to the thing to which it refers. Instead, it is another name that the compiler recognizes for the thing to which it refers.

Exercise 6-2 demonstrates the alias metaphor by displaying the addresses of both identifiers. You will see, when you run the exercise, that they both have the same address.

```
#include <iostream.h>

main()
{
    int actualint = 123;
    int& otherint = actualint;

    cout << &actualint << ' ' << &otherint;
}
```

Exercise 6-2 — Addresses of References.

Exercise 6-2 displays the following message.

`0x3b96fff4 0x3b96fff4`

Note: The format and values of these addresses will depend on where your run-time system locates the variables, and the format of the hexadecimal address in your compiler. The point here is not what the addresses are, but that they are the same.

Although the reference variable is described as an alias, it is a data item unto itself and not the same as the true alias that you could get by using the preprocessor's **#define** statement. The purpose of the reference is to gain the advantages of a pointer without requiring the associated pointer de-referencing notation. While a reference apparently delivers the behavior of a **#define**d alias, it is in fact a separate variable. It is variable because, at different times in the execution of a program, the reference can be initialized to refer to different objects.

You Must Initialize a Reference

A reference is of no use until it refers to something. Unlike a pointer, a reference is not a variable that you can manipulate. It is, as you learned in the first two exercises in this chapter, an alias for something real. Therefore, it is only natural that you must initialize a reference (explicitly give the reference something to refer to) when you declare it, unless:

1. It is declared with **extern**, in which case it would have been initialized elsewhere.

2. It is a member of a class, in which case it will be initialized in the constructor function of the class (Chapter 7).

3. It is being declared as a parameter in a function declaration, in which case its value is established by the caller's argument when the function is called.

4. It is declared as the return type of a function, in which case its value is established when the function returns something.

As you work through the exercises in this and later chapters, observe all uses of references to see that each one matches one of these criteria.

Hidden Anonymous Objects

The reference has a quirk in C++ 2.0 that can be dangerous: If the reference type differs from the type of the object you initialize it with, the compiler cannot correctly associate the reference with the object. In this case, the compiler will build a hidden anonymous object of the correct type and refer the reference to this anonymous object. While this might be what you want, it would be difficult to imagine a circumstance where you would want to do such a thing.

Exercise 6-3 illustrates the odd, but correct, behavior where a reference initialized with a different data type creates a hidden anonymous object.

```
#include <iostream.h>

main()
{
    int actualint = 123;
    long& otherint = actualint;

    cout << "\nactualint: " << actualint;
    cout << "\notherint:  " << otherint;

    cout << "\nassign 0 to otherint";
    otherint = 0;
    cout << "\nactualint: " << actualint;
    cout << "\notherint:  " << otherint;

    cout << "\nincrement otherint";
    otherint++;
    cout << "\nactualint: " << actualint;
    cout << "\notherint:  " << otherint;

    cout << "\nincrement actualint";
    actualint++;
    cout << "\nactualint: " << actualint;
    cout << "\notherint:  " << otherint;
}
```

Exercise 6-3 — Anonymous Objects.

In Exercise 6-3, an **int** named **actualint** was declared and initialized with the value 123. Then the program declares a **long** reference named **otherint** and initializes it to refer to the **int**. This causes the compiler to secretly build an anonymous **long** that has the value 123. The **otherint** reference refers to this nameless **long** variable.

Exercise 6-3 displays the following output, and as you can see, the two identifiers **actualint** and **otherint** are separate variables:

```
actualint: 123
otherint:  123
assign Ø to otherint
actualint: 123
otherint:  Ø
increment otherint
actualint: 123
otherint:  1
increment actualint
actualint: 124
otherint:  1
```

The effect of this behavior is not likely to be what was intended. It is more likely that you inadvertently used the wrong integer type on one of the declarations. The potential for this to happen is higher when the two declarations are far apart, a natural situation given the way most programmers would want to use references.

C++ version 2.1 removes this quirk from the language. The declaration of **otherint** in Exercise 6-3 is not valid in C++ 2.1 because **otherint** is not a **const**. If it were, you would not be able to assign to or increment it as the exercise does.

There is one case in C++ 2.0 where anonymous objects are more benign: The C++ 2.0 compiler generates a hidden anonymous object when you initialize a reference with a constant.

Exercise 6-4 illustrates a reference initialized with a constant. There is no named data item for the reference to refer to, so the compiler generates a hidden anonymous constant.

```
#include <iostream.h>

main()
{
    int& otherint = 123;

    cout << '\n' << otherint;
    otherint++;
    cout << '\n' << otherint;
}
```

Exercise 6-4 — Anonymous Objects from Constants.

Exercise 6-4 displays this message.

```
123
124
```

By initializing the reference with a constant, you are telling the compiler to build an anonymous object. You would do this if you wanted a distant function to modify your local variable, but you had no variable for it to modify. That is a far-fetched reason to use such a construct, but some programmers do it that way.

> Exercise 6-4 will not compile with some implementations of C++ 2.1. Initialization of a reference with a constant is no longer permitted effective with C++ version 2.1, although some CFRONT 2.1 programs still allow the practice.

References Work Best with User-defined Data Types

The odd behavior demonstrated in Exercise 6-3 is why you should generally restrict your use of references to structures and C++ classes (discussed in Chapter 7) and avoid references to the standard C++ data types. The same potential exists with your types for anonymous objects, but you are less likely to find it when referring to named data types of your own design.

References are not as helpful to you when they refer to **ints**, **longs**, and the like. As you will soon learn, a primary advantage of references is that they reduce the overhead involved with passing parameters to functions. This advantage does not exist when references to the smaller data types are present, because it takes no longer to pass the original data type than it does to pass a reference.

An exception to this practice is the use of references as returned values from functions. A later section in this chapter addresses that usage where there is benefit derived from references to **chars**, **longs**, and the like.

References as Function Parameters

References serve well as function parameters. There is little need to build a reference that exists only in the view of the variable that it refers to. You might just as well use the original name of the variable. The exercises you have seen so far have used references in that way, but the purpose of those exercises was to show you the behavior of references, not necessarily the best way to use them. Now that you understand that, you can consider how references might be useful to you.

References as function parameters offer three advantages:

1. They eliminate the overhead associated with passing large data structures as parameters.

2. They eliminate the pointer de-referencing notation used when you pass pointers to large data structures.

3. They provide for true call-by-reference parameter passing where the called function operates on the caller's copy of the data.

These advantages are illustrated in the next set of exercises.

References Improve Parameter-passing Overhead

By using a reference as a function parameter, you avoid the overhead of passing large structures to functions, much the same way you do when you pass pointers to functions.

Exercise 6-5 illustrates the difference between passing a structure and passing a reference to a structure.

```cpp
#include <iostream.h>

// ---------- a big structure
struct bigone     {
    int serno;
    char text[1000];     // a lot of chars
} bo = { 123, "This is a BIG structure"};

// -- two functions that have the structure as a
parameter
void slowfunc(bigone p1);        // call by value
void fastfunc(bigone& p1);       // call by reference

main()
{
    slowfunc(bo);    // this will take a while
    fastfunc(bo);    // this will be a snap
}

// ---- a call-by-value function
void slowfunc(bigone p1)
{
    cout << '\n' << p1.serno;
    cout << '\n' << p1.text;
}

// ---- a call by reference function
void fastfunc(bigone& p1)
{
    cout << '\n' << p1.serno;
    cout << '\n' << p1.text;
}
```

Exercise 6-5 — Reference Parameters Reduce Overhead.

Exercise 6-5 displays these messages.

```
123
This is a BIG structure
123
This is a BIG structure
```

Unfortunately, there is nothing in the exercise to prove the point. The only apparent difference is the use of the **&** reference operator in the function's prototype and parameter declaration. But the differences are real. You could find out for yourself by looking at the code that is generated for both function calls. The methods for doing that vary from compiler to compiler.

Suppose the character array in the **bigone** structure was 20,000 bytes instead of 1,000. On many systems the program would fail on the first function call because C++ passes parameters on the stack, and the stack is probably not big enough. You would need to set some implementation-dependent compiler control variable to tell the compiler that you needed a bigger stack just to support this one function call. By passing a reference to the function, you don't have to worry about it.

References Eliminate Pointer Notation

By using a reference in the called function instead of a pointer, you avoid the pointer de-referencing operators that can make pointer usage difficult to read.

Exercise 6-6 illustrates the difference between reference notation and pointer notation.

```
#include <iostream.h>

// ---------- a big structure
struct bigone    {
    int serno;
    char text[1000];    // a lot of chars
} bo = { 123, "This is a BIG structure"};

// -- two functions that have the structure as a parameter
void ptrfunc(bigone *p1);        // call by pointer
void reffunc(bigone& p1);        // call by reference

main()
{
    ptrfunc(&bo);    // pass the address
    reffunc(bo);     // pass the reference
}

// ---- a pointer function
void ptrfunc(bigone *p1)
{
    cout << '\n' << p1->serno;       // pointer notation
    cout << '\n' << p1->text;
}

// ---- a call by reference function
void reffunc(bigone& p1)
{
    cout << '\n' << p1.serno;        // reference notation
    cout << '\n' << p1.text;
}
```

Exercise 6-6 — Reference Parameters Eliminate Pointer Notation.

Exercise 6-6 displays the same messages as Exercise 6-5.

You might argue that there is little about the pointer notation in Exercise 6-6 to make it less readable than that of the reference notation. This perceived advantage is one of personal choice. The differences are more dramatic in a function with a lot of pointer de-referencing.

Call-by-reference

When one function passes a reference to another function, the called function is working on the caller's copy of the parameter, not a local copy (as it does when you pass the variable itself). This behavior is called, call-by-reference. The more conventional C parameter behavior of passing the parameter's value to a private copy in the called function is called, call-by-value.

If the called function changes a reference parameter, it is changing the caller's copy. If this is what you want, then call-by-reference works for you.

Exercise 6-7 shows how reference parameters allow a **swapper** function to swap the parameters of the caller.

```
#include <iostream.h>

// ------ simple date class
struct Date {
    int da, mo, yr;
    void display(void);
};
void Date::display()
{
    cout << da << '/' << mo << '/' << yr;
}
void swapper(Date&, Date&);
void display(Date&, Date&);

main()
{
    static Date now  = {23,2,90};    // two dates
    static Date then = {10,9,60};

    display(now, then);        // display the dates
    swapper(now, then);        // swap them
    display(now, then);        // display them swapped
}

// ----- this function swaps the caller's dates
void swapper(Date& dt1, Date& dt2)
{
    Date save;
    save = dt1;
    dt1 = dt2;
    dt2 = save;
}

void display(Date& now, Date& then)
{
    cout << "\n Now: ";
    now.display();
    cout << "\n Then: ";
    then.display();
}
```

Exercise 6-7 — Call by Reference.

In Exercise 6-7, the first two dates were initialized with different values as local variables in the **main** function. The **swapper** function swaps those two dates. It accepts two **date** references and swaps them by using simple assignment statements. Because the parameters are references, the swapping occurs to the **main** function's copy of the structures.

Exercise 6-7 displays the following date formats:

```
Now:   23/2/90
Then:  10/9/60
Now:   10/9/60
Then:  23/2/90
```

When to Use Pointers Instead of References

Consider Exercise 6-7 again. The call in **main** to **swapper** gives no indication that it uses references. The compiler knows to use references because that is how the function is prototyped and declared. But the programmer who writes **main** might not know that.

Given the purpose of the **swapper** function, it should be obvious that it uses references. If it did not, it would swap its own copies of the parameters, accomplishing nothing. But it might not be so obvious that other functions could change a caller's copy of a parameter. If the prototype is in a header file and the function is in an object library or a separately compiled source module, the reader gets no clue from the code about what is going to happen when the function gets called.

In cases like this, you are better off using a pointer. If the calling code does not pass the address of the parameter, then the reader can assume that the function will not modify the parameter. If the call passes an address, the reader can see the possibility that the parameter could be changed. The first assumption is valid only if the reader knows about the coding convention that is suggested here and if the programmer always complies with it. Nothing in C++ prevents you from disregarding such conventions and not telling anybody.

Returning a Reference

You have seen how you can pass a reference to a function as a parameter. You can also return a reference from a function. When a function returns a reference, the function call can exist in any context where a reference can exist, including the receiving side of an assignment.

Exercise 6-8 calls a function to select from an **array of dates**.

```
#include <iostream.h>
#include <stdlib.h>

// ---------- a date structure
struct Date {
    int mo, da, yr;
};

// -------- an array of dates
Date birthdays[] = {
    {12, 17, 37},
    {10, 31, 38},
    { 6, 24, 40},
    {11, 23, 42},
    { 8,  5, 44},
};

// ----- a function to retrieve a date
Date& getdate(int n)
{
    return birthdays[n-1];
}

main(int argc, char *argv[])
{
    if (argc > 1)    {
        Date& bd = getdate(atoi(argv[1]));
        cout << bd.mo << '/' << bd.da << '/' << bd.yr;
    }
}
```

Exercise 6-8 — Returning a Reference from a Function.

Exercise 6-8 displays a different date depending on the command line option, which must be 1–5. Following are the messages displayed on a PC. The first line of each pair is the MS-DOS command line prompt and the program command you enter. The second line is the date that the exercise displays.

```
C>ex06008 1
12/17/37
C>ex06008 2
10/31/38
C>ex06008 3
6/24/40
C>ex06008 4
11/23/42
C>ex06008 5
8/5/44
```

You must not return a reference to an automatic variable. The code in the following example is not legal:

```
date& getdate(void)
{
    date dt = {6, 24, 40};
    return dt;   // bad-reference to auto variable
}
```

The problem is that the **dt** variable goes out of scope when the function returns. You would, therefore, be returning a reference to a variable that no longer exists, and the calling program would be referring to a date that does not exist. Some C++ compilers issue a warning when they see code that returns references to automatic variables. If you ignore the warning, you will get unpredictable results. Sometimes the program will appear to work because the stack location where the automatic variable existed is intact when the reference is used. A program that appears to work will fail at other times due to device or multitasking interrupts that use the stack.

Note that a program that calls a function that returns a variable might not know whether the function returns a whole variable or a reference. The compiler will make the determination and generate appropriate code in either case.

Things You Cannot Do with References

There is a tendency among C++ programmers who are making the transition from C to think of references as pointer forms rather than aliases. Here again is the list of things that you cannot do to a reference.

- Point to them
- Take the address of one
- Compare them
- Assign to them
- Do arithmetic to them
- Modify them

When you try to do one of these things, you might think you are getting away with it because the compiler does not complain. Chances are the operation you are trying to apply to the reference is being applied to what the reference refers to. If you try to increment a reference, you will increment what it refers to if its data type accepts the increment operator. If you take the address of a reference, you are really taking the address of what the reference refers to.

All you can do with the reference itself is pass it to a function and return it from a function. Everything else is done to what the reference refers to, not to the reference.

Summary

The reference is a handy way to optimize your program by eliminating the overhead associated with moving large structures around in memory. You will use the reference variable extensively when you build C++ classes (see Chapter 7).

Chapter 7

Classes

C++ is, as at least one wit observed, a classy programming language. Before coming up with its present name, Dr. Stroustrup called C++, "C with classes". Classes support the way you use C++ for object-oriented programming, and they are the way you build new data types into the language. These two activities have a lot in common.

You will learn about object-oriented programming later, or perhaps you will fall into it naturally as a by-product of learning about C++. For now, however, think of classes as the means for extending C++ by designing and implementing new data types.

Designing a Class

Consider the basic numeric data types that C and C++ use. There are several types of integers and floating-point numbers. These suffice for most of your numerical needs, but there are times when the basic types need to be expanded. In C, you would traditionally organize the basic types into a logical structure and write functions to manipulate that structure. With C++, you do the same thing, but you also bind the data description and its algorithms together and set the combination up as a new data type by defining a class. The class in C++ is a data type defined by the programmer. The class consists of a user-defined data structure, member functions, and, as you will learn in Chapter 8, custom operators.

Class Definition

A class resembles the structure you learned about in Chapter 5. The class is distinguished from the C structure by its ability to hide some of its members from the rest of the program. Exercise 7-1 is an example of a class that describes the geometrical cube form.

Before proceeding to Exercise 7-1 ask yourself why you might want to build a class that describes a cube. Perhaps you are writing a program that deals with cubic containers of one kind or another, and the cube is a basic unit that the program must deal with. Any data entity that your program might process is a candidate to be a class in C++.

Exercise 7-1 illustrates classes by defining the **Cube** class.

```
#include <iostream.h>

// ------------ a Cube class
class Cube    {
private:
    int height, width, depth;    // private data members
public:
    Cube(int, int, int); // constructor function
    ~Cube();             // destructor function
    int volume(void);    // member function (compute volume)
};
// ---------- the constructor function
Cube::Cube(int ht, int wd, int dp)
{
    height = ht;
    width = wd;
    depth = dp;
}
// ---------- the destructor function
Cube::~Cube()
{
    // does nothing
}
// -------- member function to compute the Cube's volume
int Cube::volume()
{
    return height * width * depth;
}

// ========== an application to use the cube
main()
{
    Cube thiscube(7, 8, 9);      // declare a Cube
    cout << thiscube.volume();   // compute & display volume
}
```

Exercise 7-1 — The **Cube** *Class.*

Exercise 7-1 displays the cube's volume, which is 504.

There are a lot of new C++ features packed into Exercise 7-1. The program begins by defining the **Cube** class. The **Cube** has three private data members, the integers **height**, **width**, and **depth**, and three public functions, **Cube**, **~Cube**, and **volume**.

Class Declaration

A class definition only defines the class. It does not set aside any memory to hold any instance of the class. No instance of the class exists until a program declares one. This definition/declaration relationship works just like that of a structure. Exercise 7-1 declares an instance of the **Cube** class named **thiscube** in the **main** function. An instance of a class is called an object. Therefore, **thiscube** is an object of type **Cube**.

The declaration of a class object can contain a list of initializers in parentheses. The declaration of **thiscube** contains three integer values. These values will be passed to the class's constructor function, described soon.

Class Members

A class is a souped-up structure. As such, it has members, just as a structure does. A class's members are defined in the class's definition and consist of data members, the constructor and destructor functions, and member functions.

Class member visibility

The **private** and **public** access specifiers in the class definition specify the visibility of the members that follow the access specifiers. The mode invoked by an access specifier continues until another access specifier occurs or the class definition ends. Private members can be accessed only by member functions. Public members can be accessed by member functions and by other functions that declare an instance of the class. There are exceptions to these general rules. The discussion on the **friend** function later will address those exceptions.

The **Cube** class, therefore, specifies that its three integer data members are visible only to the constructor and destructor functions and to the **volume** member function, all three of which are visible to outside functions. You can use the **private** and **public** access specifiers as often as you want in a class definition, but most programmers group the private and public members separately.

All class definitions begin with the **private** access specifier as the default mode, so you could omit it in Exercise 7-1. The exercise includes it for readability and to demonstrate its purpose.

A third access specifier, the **protected** keyword, works the same as the **private** keyword except when you use class inheritance (which you will learn about in Chapter 9). For now, you will not use the **protected** access specifier.

The convention that most C++ programmers follow is represented in Exercise 7-1. When designing a class, make the data members private and the member functions public. If you need to view or modify a private data value, do it with a public member function set up for that purpose. This convention is not a rule, and there will be times when you will find it necessary to do otherwise. But if you use the convention as a guideline, your programs will be more readable.

Data members

The data members of the class are the ones that are data types. A data member may be any valid C++ data type including another class. The **Cube** class has three data members, the integers **height**, **width**, and **depth**.

The constructor function

When an instance of a class comes into scope, a special function called the constructor executes. It does, that is, if you have defined one. You define the constructor when you define the class. The **Cube** class has a constructor function named **Cube**. Constructor functions always have the same name as the class.

The run-time system provides enough memory to contain the data members of a class when the class comes into scope. The system does not initialize the data members. The class's constructor function must do any initialization that the class requires. The data variable memory goes back to the system when the class goes out of scope.

The constructor function initializes the class object. The **Cube** constructor function in Exercise 7-1 accepts three integer parameters and uses these parameters to load the data members with values that describe the **Cube**.

Observe the declaration of **thiscube** in Exercise 7-1. It follows the C syntax for declaring a variable. First comes the data type — **Cube** in this case — then comes the name of the object, **thiscube**. That's the same way you would declare an **int**, for example. But the declaration of a class object can contain an argument list in parentheses as well. This list represents class object initializers and contains the arguments that are passed to the constructor function. There must be a constructor function in the class definition with a parameter list of data types that match those of the argument list in the class object declaration.

If the constructor function has a void or empty parameter list, the declaration of the object does not require the parentheses.

A constructor function returns nothing. You do not declare it as void, but it is void by default.

You may define multiple, overloaded constructor functions for a class. Each of these would have a distinct parameter list. There will be more discussion of this feature later.

The destructor function

When a class object goes out of scope, a special function called the destructor is called. You define the destructor when you define the class. The destructor function name is always that of the class with a tilde character (~) as a prefix.

There is only one destructor function for a class. A destructor function takes no parameters and returns nothing.

The destructor function for the **Cube** class does nothing. Exercise 7-1 includes it to show its format. You could omit it altogether and get the same result. You will learn more about destructors later in this chapter.

Member functions

The member functions of the class are the functions that are declared within the class definition. You must provide the code for these functions just as you did for the functions in structures in Chapter 5.

There are several categories of functions that can appear in a class. The constructor and destructor are two of them. The others are member functions, and they can be regular members of the class, or **friend**, or **virtual** functions. You will learn about **friend** and **virtual** functions later. For now, observe that the **Cube** class has one member function, named **volume**, which is neither **friend** nor **virtual**. You name member functions in the same way you do the functions that are associated with structures and attach the class name to the function name with the **::** operator, as shown in Chapter 5. The name of the **volume** function is, therefore, **Cube::volume**.

The **Cube** class's **volume** function returns the product of the **Cube**'s three dimensions. The program in Exercise 7-1 calls the **volume** function by using the same convention for calling a structure's function. Use the structure member notation with the period operator as illustrated in the following example:

```
int vol = thiscube.volume();
```

You can call the **volume** member function anywhere an object of type **Cube** is in scope. Member functions of a class can call one another as well by using the function name without a prefix. The compiler assumes that the call is being made for the same object that the calling member function was called for.

A member function could be **private**, in which case only other member functions within the same class could call it.

The Scope of a Class Object

A class object is like any other data type with respect to scope. It comes into scope when the program declares it, and it goes out of scope when the program exits the block in which the class object is declared.

An **extern** class comes into scope when the program begins and goes out of scope when the program ends.

If you give a local class object the **static** keyword, its scope appears to be the same as an automatic object, but its actual existence is the same as that of an **extern** object. This becomes a matter to consider because C++ classes involve those special functions called the **constructor** and **destructor** functions.

inline **Functions**

A class can have **inline** functions. You learned about regular **inline** functions in Chapter 2. The same rules apply when you decide whether a class member function should be **inline**. **Inline** functions should be small.

There is a special notation for defining **inline** functions for a class. You code the body of the function directly into the class definition rather than coding a prototype. Both the **Cube** constructor function and the **Cube**'s volume member function are small enough to be **inline** functions. By coding them as **inline** and removing the unnecessary destructor function, you can significantly reduce the size of the program's source code.

Exercise 7-2 illustrates a class member function coded to be an inline member function.

```
#include <iostream.h>

// ----------- a Cube class
class Cube    {
    int height, width, depth;      // private data members
public:
    // ------ inline constructor function
    Cube(int ht, int wd, int dp)
        { height = ht; width = wd; depth = dp; }
    // ----- inline member function
    int volume()
        { return height * width * depth; }
};

main()
{
    Cube thiscube(7, 8, 9);      // declare a Cube
    cout << thiscube.volume();   // compute & display volume
}
```

Exercise 7-2 — The **Cube** *Class with* **inline** *Functions.*

Exercise 7-2 displays the cube's volume, which is 504.

You will often see **inline** class functions coded on a single line. This convention reinforces the idea that **inline** functions should be small. If you cannot get the function's body on a single line, then perhaps the function should not be an **inline** one.

Constructors with Default Arguments

Perhaps you want to initialize a **Cube** with dimensions as you did in Exercise 7-1, but at other times you want a **Cube** with default dimensions.

Exercise 7-3 shows a **Cube** class that defaults to specified dimensions if you do not supply initializers.

```
#include <iostream.h>

// ------------ a Cube class
class Cube    {
    int height, width, depth;       // private data members
public:
    // ----- constructor function with default initializers
    Cube(int ht = 1, int wd = 2, int dp = 3)
        { height = ht; width = wd; depth = dp; }
    // ----- member function
    int volume() { return height * width * depth; }
};

main()
{
    Cube thiscube(7, 8, 9);       // declare a Cube
    Cube defaultcube;             // no initializers
    cout << thiscube.volume();    // volume of the Cube
    cout << '\n';
    cout << defaultcube.volume(); // volume of the default
}
```

Exercise 7-3 — Constructor with Default Parameters.

Exercise 7-3 displays the initialized cube's volume, which is 504, followed by the default cube's volume, which is 6.

Overloaded Constructors

A class can have more than one constructor function. The several constructor functions for a class must have different parameter lists with respect to the number and types of parameters so the compiler can tell them apart. You would code multiple constructors in cases where the declarations of a class can occur with different initialization parameters. Perhaps you want to initialize a **Cube** with dimensions as you did in Exercise 7-1, but at other times you simply want an empty **Cube** with no initial dimensions; for example, to be on the receiving end of an assignment.

Exercise 7-4 shows the **Cube** with two constructor functions.

```cpp
#include <iostream.h>

// ------------ a Cube class
class Cube    {
    int height, width, depth;      // private data members
public:
    // ------ constructor functions
    Cube() { /* does nothing */ }
    Cube(int ht, int wd, int dp)
        { height = ht; width = wd; depth = dp; }
    // ----- member function
    int volume() { return height * width * depth; }
};

main()
{
    Cube thiscube(7, 8, 9);      // declare a Cube
    Cube othercube;              // a Cube with no initializers
    othercube = thiscube;
    cout << othercube.volume();
}
```

Exercise 7-4 — A Class with Two Constructors.

Exercise 7-4 displays the cube's volume, which is 504, on the screen.

This exercise uses the simplest of differences between constructors where one constructor has initializers and the other one does not. The differences between constructors can be much greater depending on the types of the class's data members and the algorithms that associate with the constructor function. You will see more complex constructor functions in later chapters.

Class Conversions

Use of C++ data types involves the implicit application of type conversion rules. If you use an **int** variable where the compiler expects a **long** variable, for example, the compiler invokes one of the type conversion rules to convert the original integer value to the new **long** format. Such conversions already exist for all pairs of data types that are compatible with respect to conversions. These implicit conversions come into play in assignments, function arguments, return values, initializers, and expressions.

Conversion Functions

You can build the same kind of implicit conversions into your classes by building conversion functions. When you write a function that converts any data type to a class, you tell the compiler to use the conversion function when the syntax of a statement implies that the conversion should take effect; that is, when the compiler expects an object of the class and sees the other data type instead.

There are two ways to write a conversion function. The first is to write a special constructor function; the second is to write a member conversion function.

Constructor conversion functions

A constructor function that has only one entry in its parameter list is a conversion function. It will work in the usual way as a constructor when you declare an object of the class type with a matching initializer argument. It will be a conversion function if you use the argument type in the syntax where the class type is expected.

You use the constructor conversion function to convert from a different data type to the class in which you define the constructor conversion function.

For these exercises, you will work with the **Date** class that stores its values as an integer for each of the elements month, day, and year.

Exercise 7-5 demonstrates a constructor conversion function that converts the value returned by the standard **time** function to the **Date** class.

```
#include <iostream.h>
#include <time.h>

class Date {
    int mo, da, yr;
public:
    Date() {}         // null constructor
    Date(time_t);     // constructor conversion function
    void display(void);
};
// ----- member function to display the date
void Date::display()
{
    cout << mo << '/' << da << '/' << yr;
}
// ------ constructor conversion function
Date::Date(time_t now)
{
    struct tm *tim = localtime(&now);
    da = tim->tm_mday;
    mo = tim->tm_mon + 1;
    yr = tim->tm_year;
}

main()
{
    time_t now = time((time_t *)NULL); // today's date and time
    Date dt(now);     // invoke the conversion constructor
    dt.display();     // display today's date
}
```

Exercise 7-5 — Constructor Conversion Function.

Exercise 7-5 displays the current date in month/day/year format, for example, 5/3/91.

Member conversion functions

You use a member conversion function to convert from the class in which you define it to a different data type. A member conversion function uses the C++ **operator** keyword in its declaration. This usage is your first exposure to C++ **operator** overloading, the subject of Chapter 8. To declare a member conversion function within a class, you code its prototype as illustrated by the following example:

```
operator long();
```

The **long** in this example is the type specifier of the converted data type. The type specifier can be any valid C++ type, including another class. You would define the member conversion function with the following notation:

```
Classname::operator long()
```

The **Classname** identifier is the type specifier of the class in which the function is declared and from which you will convert to get the **long**. The function must return the data type to which it is converting, in this case a **long**.

There is not enough information in the **Date** class to convert it back to the **time_t** variable, but you can convert it to, for example, a **long** integer containing the number of days since the beginning of the century.

Exercise 7-6 shows how you would use a member function to make the conversion.

```
#include <iostream.h>

class Date {
    int mo, da, yr;
public:
    Date(int m, int d, int y) { mo = m; da = d; yr = y; }
    operator long();    // member conversion function
};

// ---- the member conversion function
Date::operator long()
{
    static int dys[]={31,28,31,30,31,30,31,31,30,31,30,31};
    long days = yr;
    days *= 365;
    days += yr / 4;
    for (int i = 0; i < mo-1; i++)
        days += dys[i];
    days += da;
    return days;
}

main()
{
    Date xmas(12, 25, 89);
    long since = xmas;
    cout << '\n' << since;
}
```

Exercise 7-6 — Conversion Member Function.

Exercise 7-6 displays the number 32866, which is the number of days from the turn of the century until Christmas of 1989.

Converting Classes

The conversion examples so far have converted a class to and from a fixed C++ data type. You can also define conversion functions that convert from one class to another.

Exercise 7-7 shows you how to convert classes.

```
#include <iostream.h>

// -------- Julian date class
class Julian {
public:
    int da, yr;
    Julian() {}
    Julian(int d, int y) { da = d; yr = y;}
    void display(){ cout << '\n' << yr << '-' << da; }
};

// ------- date class
class Date {
    int mo, da, yr;
public:
    Date() {}
    Date(int m, int d, int y) { mo = m; da = d; yr = y; }
    Date(Julian);          // constructor conversion function
    operator Julian();     // member conversion function
    void display(){cout << '\n' << mo << '/' << da
                        << '/' << yr;}
};
```

Exercise 7-7 continued...

…from previous page

```
static int dys[] = {31,28,31,30,31,30,31,31,30,31,30,31};

// -- constructor conversion function (Date <- Julian)
Date::Date(Julian jd)
{
    yr = jd.yr;
    da = jd.da;
    for (mo = 0; mo < 11; mo++)
        if (da > dys[mo])
            da -= dys[mo];
        else
            break;
    mo++;
}

// ---- member conversion function (Julian <- Date)
Date::operator Julian()
{
    Julian jd(0, yr);
    for (int i = 0; i < mo-1; i++)
        jd.da += dys[i];
    jd.da += da;
    return jd;
}

main()
{
    Date dt(11,17,89);
    Julian jd;
    // ------- convert Date to Julian
    jd = dt;
    jd.display();
    // ------- convert Julian to Date
    dt = jd;
    dt.display();
}
```

Exercise 7-7 — Converting Classes.

Exercise 7-7 displays the two converted date formats as shown here.

```
89-321
11/17/89
```

This exercise has two classes, a **Julian** date and a **Date**. A **Julian** date is one that contains the year and the day of the year from 1 to 365. The conversion functions in Exercise 7-7 convert between the two date formats.

> The date conversion algorithms in these exercises do not consider things such as the millennium or the leap year. These omissions are intentional to keep the exercises as simple as possible.

Both kinds of conversion functions are built into the **Date** class in Exercise 7-7. This approach works because you convert from the **Date** type to the **Julian** type with the member conversion function and from the **Julian** type to the **Date** type with the constructor conversion function.

Note that it would not be legal to have a **Date** to **Julian** member conversion function in the **Date** class and a **Date** to **Julian** constructor conversion function in the **Julian** class. This circumstance would confuse the compiler about which function to call to perform the conversion.

Invoking conversion functions

There are three C++ forms that invoke a conversion function. The first is the implicit conversion that you have seen so far in the exercises. For example, where the compiler expects to see a **Date** and the program supplies a **Julian**, the compiler will call the appropriate conversion function. The other two forms involve explicit conversions that you write into the code. These conversions resemble the C++ cast.

Exercise 7-8 illustrates the three class conversion forms.

```
#include <iostream.h>

// -------- Julian date class
class Julian {
public:
    int da, yr;
    Julian() {}
    Julian(int d, int y) { da = d; yr = y;}
    void display(){cout << '\n' << yr << '-' << da;}
};

// ------- date class
class Date {
    int mo, da, yr;
public:
    Date(int m, int d, int y) { mo = m; da = d; yr = y; }
    operator Julian(); // conversion function
};

static int dys[] = {31,28,31,30,31,30,31,31,30,31,30,31};

// ---- member conversion function (Julian <- Date)
Date::operator Julian()
{
    Julian jd(0, yr);
    for (int i = 0; i < mo-1; i++)
        jd.da += dys[i];
    jd.da += da;
    return jd;
}
```

Exercise 7-8 continued...

...from previous page

```
main()
{
    Date dt(11,17,89);
    Julian jd;
    // ------- convert Date to Julian via implicit conversion
    jd = dt;
    jd.display();
    // ------- convert Date to Julian via cast
    jd = (Julian) dt;
    jd.display();
    // ------- convert Date to Julian via reverse cast
    jd = Julian(dt);
    jd.display();
}
```

Exercise 7-8 — Invoking Conversions.

Exercise 7-8 displays the three Julian dates that were converted from conventional dates in three ways as shown here.

```
89-321
89-321
89-321
```

> Note that a bug in the Zortech 2.1 compiler prevents the third form from working correctly. This bug has been there since version 2.0.

The contexts where conversions occur

So far the exercises have invoked conversion functions by assigning one class to another. The following list identifies several other contexts in which a conversion function comes into play:

- As a function argument
- As an initializer
- As a return value
- In an expression.

105

Exercise 7-9 illustrates some of the ways you can cause a conversion function to be called.

```
#include <iostream.h>

// -------- Julian date class
class Julian {
public:
    int da, yr;
    Julian() {}
    Julian(int d, int y) { da = d; yr = y;}
    void display(){cout << '\n' << yr << '-' << da;}
};

// ------- date class
class Date {
    int mo, da, yr;
public:
    Date(int m, int d, int y) { mo = m; da = d; yr = y; }
    operator Julian(); // conversion function
};

// ----- a class that expects a Julian date as an initializer
class Tester {
    Julian jd;
public:
    Tester(Julian j) { jd = j; }
    void display() { jd.display(); }
};

static int dys[] = {31,28,31,30,31,30,31,31,30,31,30,31};

// ---- member conversion function (Julian <- Date)
Date::operator Julian()
{
    Julian jd(0, yr);
```

Exercise 7-9 continued...

...from previous page

```
    for (int i = 0; i < mo-1; i++)
        jd.da += dys[i];
    jd.da += da;
    return jd;
}

// -------- a function that expects a Julian date
void dispdate(Julian jd)
{
    jd.display();
}

// --------- a function that returns a Julian Date
Julian rtndate()
{
    Date dt(10,11,88);
    return dt;              // this will be converted to Julian
}

main()
{
    Date dt(11,17,89);
    Julian jd;
    // ------- convert Date to Julian via assignment
    jd = dt;
    jd.display();
    // ------- convert Date to Julian via function argument
    dispdate(dt);
    // ------- convert Date to Julian via initializer
    Tester ts(dt);
    ts.display();
    // ------- convert Date to Julian via return value
    jd = rtndate();
    jd.display();
}
```

Exercise 7-9 — Contexts for Conversions.

Exercise 7-9 displays the Julian dates converted from four different program contexts as shown here.

```
89-321
89-321
89-321
88-284
```

Conversion within an expression occurs in those expressions where one type is expected and another type is found. You can see this process more readily when the conversion is to a numeric type instead of another class.

Exercise 7-10 uses the earlier conversion of a date to a **long** integer to illustrate how the integral representation of a class can, through conversion, contribute directly to an expression.

```cpp
#include <iostream.h>

class Date {
    int mo, da, yr;
public:
    Date(int m, int d, int y) { mo = m; da = d; yr = y; }
    operator long();     // member conversion function
};

// ---- the member conversion function
Date::operator long()
{
    static int dys[]={31,28,31,30,31,30,31,31,30,31,30,31};
    long days = yr;
    days *= 365;
    days += yr / 4;
    for (int i = 0; i < mo-1; i++)
        days += dys[i];
    days += da;
    return days;
}
```

Exercise 7-10 continued...

...from previous page

```
main()
{
    Date today(2, 12, 90);
    const long ott = 123;
    long sum = ott + today;      // today is converted to long
    cout << ott << " + " << (long) today << " = " << sum;
}
```

Exercise 7-10 — Conversion in an Expression.

Exercise 7-10 displays this expression.

```
123 + 32915 = 33038
```

The implicit conversion from within an expression will occur for a class-to-class conversion if the converted class can appear in a conversion; that is, if the converted class can itself be converted to a numerical type, or if the expression invokes an overloaded operator that works with the class. Chapter 8 discusses overloading operators.

Manipulating Private Data Members

All the data members in the **Julian** class in Exercises 7-7, 7-8, and 7-9 are public. This approach allows the conversion functions in the **Date** class to read and write the data members of the **Julian** object. Making the members public is one way to allow this access, but when you do, you make the members public to all other functions as well. You might not want to do that. Remember the convention for keeping the data members private and the member functions public. These exercises violated that convention to get their point across. Now you should consider alternative ways to get the same results within the bounds of the accepted conventions.

As a general rule, you make all the data members private and you provide member functions to read and write them.

Exercise 7-11 shows how the **Date** class can have member functions that provide controlled access to the data members.

```
#include <iostream.h>

class Date {
    int mo, da, yr;
public:
    Date(int m, int d, int y) { mo = m; da = d; yr = y; }
    // ---- a member function to return the year
    int getyear() { return yr; }
    // ---- a member function to allow the year to be changed
    int& year() { return yr; }
};

main()
{
    // -------- set up a Date
    Date dt(4, 1, 89);
    // ------- use a member function to read the year value
    cout << "\nThe year is: " << dt.getyear();
    // ------ use a member function to change the year
    dt.year() = 90;
    cout << "\nThe new year is: " << dt.getyear();
}
```

Exercise 7-11 — Manipulating Data Members Though Member Functions.

Exercise 7-11 displays these messages.

```
The year is: 89
The new year is: 90
```

By consistently using this approach, you ensure that accesses and changes to the data of a class are managed by the member functions that are bound to the class. This binding strengthens a software design and makes it easier to maintain.

Observe that the year member function in Exercise 7-11 returns a reference. Because the function returns a reference, you can use the function call on the left side of an assignment the way the exercise shows.

With that simple example as an introduction, you are ready to apply the technique to an earlier problem.

Exercise 7-12 uses the member function access technique to improve the code in the conversion function that converts a **Date** object to a **Julian** object.

```
#include <iostream.h>

// -------- Julian date class
class Julian {
    int da, yr;
public:
    Julian() {}
    Julian(int d, int y) { da = d; yr = y;}
    void display(){cout << '\n' << yr << '-' << da;}
    // ------ member function to read and write a day
    int& day() { return da; }
};


// ------- date class
class Date {
    int mo, da, yr;
public:
    Date(int m, int d, int y) { mo = m; da = d; yr = y; }
    operator Julian(); // conversion function
};

static int dys[] = {31,28,31,30,31,30,31,31,30,31,30,31};
// ---- member conversion function (Julian <- Date)
Date::operator Julian()
{
    Julian jd(0, yr);
    for (int i = 0; i < mo-1; i++)
        jd.day() += dys[i];         // uses member function to
    jd.day() += da;          // change da in Julian class
    return jd;
}
main()
{
    Date dt(11,17,89);
    Julian jd;
    // ------- convert Date to Julian via assignment
    jd = dt;
    jd.display();
}
```

Exercise 7-12 — Conversions with Proper Data Hiding.

Exercise 7-12 displays this converted Julian Date

89-321

Friends

Having learned that hidden access to data members is best, you must now consider the exceptions to that rule. There are times when a class definition must allow outside functions to directly read and write the class's data members.

As an example, the technique you just learned involves calling a function every time you want access to a particular data member of a class. The member functions that granted the access in the exercises were **inline** functions, so the overhead involved in their use is minimal. But if such an access requires enough processing that an **inline** function is impractical, then each read or write of a data member involves the overhead associated with a call to a function. In this case, you could encode the accessing function as a **friend** to the class where the data item is a member.

The **friend** keyword in a class, specifies that a function or all the member functions of another class can read and write the original class's private data members.

Friend Classes

The first kind of **friend** is the class **friend**. A class can specify that all the member functions of another class can read and write the first class's private data members by identifying the other class as a **friend**.

Exercise 7-13 illustrates the use of the **friend** class.

```
#include <iostream.h>

class Date;          // tells compiler a Date class is coming
// -------- Julian date class
class Julian {
    int da, yr;
public:
    Julian() {}
    Julian(int d, int y) { da = d; yr = y;}
    void display() {cout << '\n' << yr << '-' << da;}
    friend Date;     // allows Date member functions to see
                     // Julian private members
};
// ------- date class
class Date {
    int mo, da, yr;
public:
    Date(int m, int d, int y) { mo = m; da = d; yr = y; }
    operator Julian();
};

static int dys[] = {31,28,31,30,31,30,31,31,30,31,30,31};

// ---- member conversion function (Julian <- Date)
Date::operator Julian()
{
    Julian jd(0, yr);
    for (int i = 0; i < mo-1; i++)
        jd.da += dys[i];
    jd.da += da;
    return jd;
}

main()
{
    Date dt(11,17,89);
    Julian jd;
    jd = dt;
    jd.display();
}
```

*Exercise 7-13 — **Friend** Classes.*

114

Exercise 7-13 displays this converted Julian Date:

`89-321`

Observe this new construct in the **Julian** class of Exercise 7-13 in the following example:

`friend Date;`

This statement tells the compiler that member functions of the **Date** class have access to the private members of the **Julian** class. The conversion functions of the **Date** class need to see the individual data components of the **Julian** class and so the entire **Date** class is named as a **friend** of the **Julian** class.

Another new C++ construct is contained in Exercise 7-13. The beginning of the program has the following statement:

`class Date;`

This statement tells the compiler that a class named **Date** will be defined later. The compiler needs to know about that because the **Julian** class refers to the **Date** class, and the **Date** class refers to the **Julian** class. One of them must come first, so the statement serves to resolve the forward reference to **Date** that occurs in the **Julian** class.

You can eliminate the need for the **class Date;** statement by including the **class** keyword in the **friend** declaration.

Exercise 7-14 modifies the Exercise 7-13 program by using the class keyword.

```
#include <iostream.h>

// -------- Julian date class
class Julian {
    int da, yr;
public:
    Julian() {}
    Julian(int d, int y) { da = d; yr = y;}
    void display() {cout << '\n' << yr << '-' << da;}
    friend class Date;    // <- forward reference to class
};

// ------- date class
class Date {
    int mo, da, yr;
public:
    Date(int m, int d, int y) { mo = m; da = d; yr = y; }
    operator Julian();
};

static int dys[] = {31,28,31,30,31,30,31,31,30,31,30,31};

// ---- member conversion function (Julian <- Date)
Date::operator Julian()
{
    Julian jd(0, yr);
    for (int i = 0; i < mo-1; i++)
        jd.da += dys[i];
    jd.da += da;
    return jd;
}

main()
{
    Date dt(11,17,89);
    Julian jd;
    jd = dt;
    jd.display();
}
```

*Exercise 7-14 — **Friend** Classes, Forward Reference.*

Exercise 7-14 displays this converted **Julian Date**

`89-321`

Friend Functions

Usually you do not want an entire class to be a **friend** of another class. Unless it is necessary to access data in such a broad way, then you should not do so. What you need is a way to specify that only selected member functions of another class may read and write the data members of the current class. In these cases, you may specify that a particular function rather than an entire class is a friend of a class.

Exercise 7-15 restricts the access to the data members of the **Julian** class to only the member function of the **Date** class that needs it.

```
#include <iostream.h>

class Julian;
// ------- date class
class Date {
    int mo, da, yr;
public:
    Date() {}
    Date(Julian);           // constructor conversion function
    void display()
        {cout << '\n' << mo << '/' << da << '/' << yr;}
};
// -------- Julian date class
class Julian {
    int da, yr;
public:
    Julian(int d, int y) { da = d; yr = y; }
    friend Date::Date(Julian); // friend conversion function
};
static int dys[] = {31,28,31,30,31,30,31,31,30,31,30,31};
// ---- constructor conversion function (Date <- Julian)
Date::Date(Julian jd)
{
    yr = jd.yr;
    da = jd.da;
    for (mo = 0; mo < 11; mo++)
        if (da > dys[mo])
            da -= dys[mo];
        else
            break;
    mo++;
}
main()
{
    Date dt;
    Julian jd(123, 89);
    dt = jd;            // convert Julian to Date
    dt.display();
}
```

*Exercise 7-15 — **Friend** Functions in a Class.*

Exercise 7-15 displays this date converted from a Julian Date:

5/3/89

Sometimes the function that is to be a **friend** is not a member of another class at all. You may specify that a nonclass member function is a **friend** to a class. That function would then have the special privilege of reading and writing the class's private data members. This feature is particularly useful when overloading operators, the subject of Chapter 8.

A frequent use of nonmember **friend** functions is to bridge classes. A function that is **friend** to more than one class can have access to the private members of both. Suppose you have a **Time** class and a **Date** class and you want a function that displays both.

Exercise 7-16 shows how a **friend** function that has access to the data members of both classes can bridge the two.

```
#include <iostream.h>

class Time;

// ------- date class
class Date {
    int mo, da, yr;
public:
    Date(int m, int d, int y) { mo = m; da = d; yr = y;}
    friend void display(Date&, Time&); // bridge function
};

// ------- time class
class Time {
    int hr, min, sec;
public:
    Time(int h, int m, int s) { hr = h; min = m; sec = s;}
    friend void display(Date&, Time&); // bridge function
};

// -------- a bridge friend function
void display(Date& dt, Time& tm)
{
    cout << '\n' << dt.mo << '/' << dt.da << '/' << dt.yr;
    cout << ' ';
    cout << tm.hr << ':' << tm.min << ':' << tm.sec;
}

main()
{
    Date dt(2,16,90);
    Time tm(10,55,0);
    display(dt, tm);
}
```

*Exercise 7-16 — Bridging Classes with a **Friend** Function.*

Exercise 7-16 displays this date and time message:

```
2/16/90 10:55:0
```

Classes and References

Chapter 6 taught you about references. Now that you have learned about classes, you should be able to apply references and classes to one another. Everything you learned about using references with the standard C++ data types and structures applies equally to classes. The ability to pass references to class objects among functions gives a C++ program a measure of efficiency that it would not have if you had to pass every object by value.

In Exercise 7-16, you were shown references to objects of the **Date** and **Time** classes as parameters to the **display** function. Note that the calling program looks as if it is passing the objects themselves. If you do not bother to look at the prototype of the **display** function, you might not know (nor care) that the function uses references. The compiler knows, however, and correctly passes references to the function.

Destructors

Until now, the exercises in this chapter have not treated the subject of destructors because the classes in them have not required anything in the way of custom destruction. Destructors are a peculiar breed of function with their own set of problems to consider.

To begin the discussion on destructors, you will build a new **Date** class that includes a pointer to a string that contains the month spelled out.

Exercise 7-17 implements the destructor function for the **Date** class.

```
#include <iostream.h>
#include <string.h>

// ------- date class
class Date {
    int mo, da, yr;
    char *month;
public:
    Date();
    Date(int m, int d, int y);
    ~Date();
    void display();
};

// constructor that is called for an uninitialized Date
Date::Date()
{
    mo = 0; da = 0; yr = 0;
    month = NULL;
}

// constructor that is called for an initialized Date
Date::Date(int m, int d, int y)
{
    static char *mos[] = {
        "January", "February", "March", "April", "May",
        "June", "July", "August", "September", "October",
        "November", "December"
    };
    mo = m; da = d; yr = y;
    month = new char[strlen(mos[m-1])+1];
    strcpy(month, mos[m-1]);
}

// Destructor for a Date
Date::~Date()
{
    if (month != NULL)
        delete month;
}
```

Exercise 7-17 continued...

…from previous page

```
// ---------- display member function
void Date::display()
{
    if (month != NULL)
        cout << '\n' << month << ' ' << da << ", "
            << yr+1900;
}

main()
{
    Date birthday(6,24,40);
    birthday.display();
}
```

Exercise 7-17 — Destructors.

Exercise 7-17 displays this date:

`June 24, 1940`

> Note that as the member functions get bigger, they are no longer **inline** functions.

The constructor function for the uninitialized **Date** object sets all the integer data members to zero and the **month** pointer to NULL.

The constructor function for the initialized **Date** object first uses the **new** operator to allocate some free-store memory for the string name of the month. It then copies the name from its internal array into the **Date** object's **month** character pointer. Of course, you could have simply copied the pointer from the constructor's array into the class in the context of this exercise, but the point of the exercise is to discuss destructors. If you had copied the pointer, the object would have nothing that needed destroying.

The destructor function deletes the **month** pointer if it contains a non-NULL value, and this is where you can get into trouble. As programmed, the exercise has no problems, but as designed, the **Date** class can cause trouble when used in an assignment. Suppose you added the following code to the main function in Exercise 7-17:

```
Date newday;
newday = birthday;
```

You would construct an empty **Date** variable named **newday** and then assign the contents of **birthday** to it. That looks reasonable, but when you consider what the destructor function does, you will see the problem.

C++ figures that if you do not tell it otherwise, a class assignment is either a binary copy or a member-by-member copy. In this example, the **birthday** variable has **month**, a character pointer that was initialized by the constructor's use of the **new** operator. The destructor will use the **delete** operator to release the memory when **birthday** goes out of scope. But, when that happens, **newday** will go out of scope too, and the destructor will execute for it as well. The **month** pointer in **newday** is a copy of the **month** pointer in **birthday**. The constructor will **delete** the same pointer twice, giving unpredictable results, and that is a problem that you must deal with in your design of the class.

Furthermore, suppose that **newday** is an external object and **birthday** is automatic. When **birthday** goes out of scope, it deletes the **month** pointer in the **newday** object.

Now, suppose that you had two initialized **Date** variables and you assigned one to the other as in the following example:

```
Date birthday(6,24,40);
Date newday(7,29,41);
newday = birthday;
```

The problem compounds itself. When the two variables go out of scope, the **month** value originally assigned in **birthday** is in **newday** as a result of the assignment. The **month** value that the constructor's **new** operation put into **newday** has been overwritten by the assignment. Not only does the **month** value in **birthday** get deleted twice, the one that was originally in **newday** never gets deleted.

Class Assignment

The solution to this set of problems lies in recognizing when they will occur and writing a special assignment operator function to deal with them. The discussion on conversion functions earlier in this chapter introduced you to the technique for overloading the assignment operator to manage conversions between classes and other data types. You can overload the assignment operator for assigning two objects of the same class as well. It is with this technique that you solve the problem of assignment and destruction of free-store pointers in a class. (Chapter 8 discusses overloaded operators in detail.)

The technique you are about to learn is quite simple. Your class assignment function will use the new operator to get a different pointer from the free store. Then it will copy the value pointed to in the assigning object, into the area pointed to in the assigned object.

Exercise 7-18 is an example of how the class-assignment technique works.

```
// ------- date class
class Date {
    int mo, da, yr;
    char *month;
public:
    Date();
    Date(int m, int d, int y);
    ~Date();
    void operator=(Date&); // overloaded assignment operator
    void display();
};

// constructor that is called for an uninitialized Date
Date::Date()
{
    mo = 0; da = 0; yr = 0;
    month = NULL;
}

// constructor that is called for an initialized Date
Date::Date(int m, int d, int y)
{
    static char *mos[] = {
        "January", "February", "March", "April", "May",
        "June", "July", "August", "September", "October",
        "November", "December"
    };
    mo = m; da = d; yr = y;
    month = new char[strlen(mos[m-1])+1];
    strcpy(month, mos[m-1]);
}
// Destructor for a Date
Date::~Date()
{
```

Exercise 7-18 continued...

…from previous page

```
        if (month != NULL)
            delete month;
    }

    // ---------- display member function
    void Date::display()
    {
        if (month != NULL)
            cout << '\n' << month << ' ' << da << ", "
                << yr+1900;
    }

    // ---------- overloaded Date assignment
    void Date::operator=(Date& dt)
    {
        mo = dt.mo;
        da = dt.da;
        yr = dt.yr;
        if (month != NULL)
            delete month;
        if (dt.month != NULL)    {
            month = new char [strlen(dt.month)+1];
            strcpy(month, dt.month);
        }
        else
            month = NULL;
    }

    main()
    {
        // ------ first date
        Date birthday(6,24,40);
        birthday.display();
        // ------ second date
        Date newday(7,29,41);
        newday.display();
        // ------ assign first to second
        newday = birthday;
        newday.display();
    }
```

Exercise 7-18 — Class Assignment.

This exercise contains all the components of Exercise 7-17, but with the overloaded assignment operator function added to the **Date** class definition. The function makes the usual data-member assignments, then tests to see if the receiving object's **month** pointer has a non-NULL value. If so, the object has been initialized or previously assigned to, and, because of the assignment, its values are to be discarded. In that case, the function uses the **delete** operator to return the object's **month** string memory to the free store. Then, if the sending object's month pointer has been initialized (if not, the sender was never initialized), the function uses **new** to allocate memory for the receiving object and copies the sending object's **month** string to the receiver.

Exercise 7-18 displays the following messages:

```
June 24, 1940
July 29, 1941
June 24, 1940
```

You cannot always see the effects of the overloaded assignment function by observing a properly running program such as that in Exercise 7-18. The effects of leaving it out will be different from compiler to compiler. In some cases, the code might even work for a time. The effects of deleting pointers that have already been deleted are undefined, and it is perfectly correct for the compiler to generate code that crashes if you do so. The effect of *not* deleting pointers that you no longer need is that you will eventually exhaust the free store.

The this **Pointer**

The **this** pointer is a special pointer that exists for a class while a nonstatic member function is executing. The **this** pointer is a pointer to an object of the type of the class and it points to the object for which the member function is currently executing.

Note that **this** does not exist in a static member function (see the discussion on Static Members, later in this chapter).

When you call a member function for an object, the compiler assigns the address of the object to the **this** pointer and then calls the function. Therefore, every reference to a data member from within a member function implicitly uses the **this** pointer. The two output statements in the following example do the same thing.

In this example, the second statement explicitly uses the pointer notation that the first statement uses implicitly:

```
void Date::month_display()
{
    cout << mo;        // these two statements
    cout << this->mo; // do the same thing
}
```

Returning *this

One purpose of the **this** pointer is to allow member functions to return the invoking object to the caller. The overloaded assignment operator function in Exercise 7-18 returns nothing. With that function you would not be able to string assignments together in the C and C++ format as follows:

```
a = b = c;
```

Such an assignment works in C and C++ because every expression returns something, unless it is a function returning void. The preceding example can be expressed the following way:

```
b = c;
a = b;
```

Because the first statement is an expression that returns the value assigned, the two expressions can be combined as follows:

```
a = (b = c);
```

Because the rightmost assignment operator has higher precedence than the leftmost one, the parentheses are not required, and the preceding example is thus expressed the following way:

```
a = b = c;
```

To make your overloaded class assignments work the same way, you must make the assignment function return the result of the assignment, which happens to be the object being assigned to. This also happens to be what the **this** pointer points to while the assignment function is executing.

Exercise 7-19 modifies Exercise 7-18 by having the overloaded assignment function return a reference to a **Date**. The value returned is the object pointed to by the this pointer.

```cpp
#include <iostream.h>
#include <string.h>

// ------- date class
class Date {
    int mo, da, yr;
    char *month;
public:
    Date();
    Date(int m, int d, int y);
    ~Date();
    Date& operator=(Date&); //overloaded assignment operator
    void display();
};
// constructor that is called for an uninitialized Date
Date::Date()
{
    mo = 0; da = 0; yr = 0;
    month = NULL;
}
// constructor that is called for an initialized Date
Date::Date(int m, int d, int y)
{
    static char *mos[] = {
        "January", "February", "March", "April", "May",
        "June", "July", "August", "September", "October",
        "November", "December"
    };
    mo = m; da = d; yr = y;
    month = new char[strlen(mos[m-1])+1];
    strcpy(month, mos[m-1]);
}
```

Exercise 7-19 continued...

...from previous page

```
// Destructor for a Date
Date::~Date()
{
    if (month != NULL)
        delete month;
}

// ---------- display member function
void Date::display()
{
    if (month != NULL)
        cout << '\n' << month << ' ' << da << ", "
            << yr+1900;
}

// ---------- overloaded Date assignment
Date& Date::operator=(Date& dt)
{
    mo = dt.mo;
    da = dt.da;
    yr = dt.yr;
    if (month != NULL)
        delete month;
    if (dt.month != NULL)    {
        month = new char [strlen(dt.month)+1];
        strcpy(month, dt.month);
    }
    else
        month = NULL;
    return *this;
}
```

Exercise 7-19 continued...

...from previous page

```
main()
{
    // ------ original date
    Date birthday(6,24,40);
    Date oldday, newday;
    // ------ assign first to second to third
    oldday = newday = birthday;
    birthday.display();
    oldday.display();
    newday.display();
}
```

Exercise 7-19 — The **this** *Pointer.*

Exercise 7-19 displays these three dates.

```
June 24, 1940
June 24, 1940
June 24, 1940
```

This use of the **this** pointer is sometimes difficult to grasp because it applies several C++ constructs that are unfamiliar to the C programmer. Picture what is happening when you make the following assignment:

```
newday = birthday;
```

The assignment executes the overloaded assignment operator function for the **Date** class. That function has two parameters. The first parameter is implied. It is the address of the object for which the function is being called. In this case, the function is being called for the object on the left side of the assignment, the **newday** object. The second parameter is supplied as an argument and is the object on the right side of the assignment, in this case the **birthday** object. In the function, the **birthday** object becomes the **dt** parameter. The first statement in the function is as follows:

```
mo = dt.mo;
```

This statement can also be read the following way:

```
this->mo = dt.mo;
```

The statement assigns the value in the **mo** data member of the **birthday** object to the **mo** data member of the **newday** object. The other assignments work the same. When the function is done, it returns what **this** points to, the **newday** object. Because the function really returns a reference, the compiler converts the *return of* what **this** points to into a *reference to* what **this** points to. The result is that the overloaded assignment operator function, in addition to performing the assignment, returns the object that received the assignment making the following statement possible:

```
oldday = newday = birthday;
```

By understanding this mechanism and the subject of operator overloading (as discussed in Chapter 8), you can see how the chained **cout** statements used in previous exercises work. You have been using statements similar to the following example in many of the exercises:

```
cout << a << b << c;
```

Using this to Link Lists

The **this** pointer is convenient in applications where a data structure uses self-referential members. An example is the simple linked list.

Exercise 7-20 builds a linked list of a class named **ListEntry**.

```
#include <iostream.h>
#include <string.h>

class ListEntry {
    char *listvalue;
    ListEntry *preventry;
public:
    ListEntry(char *);
    ~ListEntry() { delete listvalue; }
    ListEntry *PrevEntry() { return preventry; };
    void display() { cout << '\n' << listvalue; }
    // ---------- use the 'this' pointer to chain the list
    void AddEntry(ListEntry& le) { le.preventry = this; }
};

ListEntry::ListEntry(char *s)
{
    listvalue = new char[strlen(s)+1];
    strcpy(listvalue, s);
    preventry = NULL;
}

main()
{
    ListEntry *prev = NULL;
    // ---------- read in some names
    while (1)    {
        cout << "\nEnter a name ('end' when done): ";
        char name[25];
        cin >> name;
        if (strncmp(name, "end", 3) == 0)
            break;
```

Exercise 7-20 continued...

…from previous page

```
            // --------- make a list entry of the name
            ListEntry *list = new ListEntry(name);
            if (prev != NULL)
                // --------- add the entry to the linked list
                prev->AddEntry(*list);
            prev = list;
        }
        // -------- display the names in reverse order
        while (prev != NULL)    {
            prev->display();
            ListEntry *hold = prev;
            prev = prev->PrevEntry();
            // --------- delete the ListEntry
            delete hold;
        }
    }
```

Exercise 7-20 — **this** *and the Linked List.*

Exercise 7-20 displays the following prompting messages. Enter names until you are done, then enter "end." The program displays the names in the reverse order in which you entered them.

```
Enter a name ('end' when done): Sonny
Enter a name ('end' when done): Jay
Enter a name ('end' when done): Alan
Enter a name ('end' when done): Wally
Enter a name ('end' when done): Julie
Enter a name ('end' when done): end

Julie
Wally
Alan
Jay
Sonny
```

The class in Exercise 7-20 has a string value and a pointer to the previous entry in the list. The constructor function gets memory for the string from the free store, copies the string value to the class and sets the pointer to NULL. The destructor deletes the string memory.

135

Note that if you wanted to use this class in a broader scope, to include assignments of objects of the class to one another, you would need to build an overloaded assignment operator like the one in Exercise 7-18.

A member function named **PrevEntry** returns the pointer to the previous entry in the list. Another member function displays the current entry.

The member function of concern here is the one named **AddEntry**. It builds the list by putting the address of the current entry into the pointer of the next entry. It does this by copying the **this** pointer into the **preventry** pointer of the argument entry.

The main function of the program prompts you to enter some names at the console. After the last name you should enter the word end. Then the function navigates the list and displays the entries. Because the list pointers point from the current to the previous entry, the names display in the opposite order in which you entered them.

> Note the use of the **new** operator to allocate memory for the **ListEntry** object that will be pointed to by the **list** pointer. Chapter 3 addressed **new** and **delete** but did not discuss those operators with respect to classes because you had not learned about classes. A later section in this chapter discusses the free store as it pertains to objects of classes.

How Not to Use the `this` Pointer

The **this** pointer is just like any other pointer. What it points to and its scope are dependent on the object for which the member function is called. It exists in constructor and destructor functions. You can do some tricks with **this**.

You can preempt the compiler's use of **this** in a constructor function by assigning a value to **this**. This means that you are responsible for the management of all the memory allocated for the object, including for the data members. You can assign a NULL value to **this** in a destructor function, which means that the compiler will not be able to deallocate the object's memory. You should try these tricks only if you know what you are doing and why you are doing it. As a rule of good programming, let the compiler manage the values in **this**.

Normally, an introductory tutorial such as this one would ignore the tricky aspects of a subject such as the **this** pointer, leaving them for you to discover when you have more experience. But several published works on C++ document these characteristics of **this** without adequately warning you about the perils of using them.

Arrays of Class Objects

A class object is just like any other C++ data type in that you can declare pointers to them and arrays of them. The array notation is the same as that of an array of structures.

Exercise 7-21 shows an array of **Date** structures.

```
#include <iostream.h>

// ------- date class
class Date {
    int mo, da, yr;
public:
    Date() { mo = 0; da = 0; yr = 0; }
    Date(int m, int d, int y) { mo = m; da = d; yr = y;}
    void display()
        { cout << '\n' << mo << '/' << da << '/' <<yr; }
};

main()
{
    Date dates[2];
    Date temp(6,24,40);

    dates[0] = temp;
    dates[0].display();
    dates[1].display();
}
```

Exercise 7-21 — Arrays of Classes.

The constructor function in Exercise 7-21 for declarations without initializers initializes the three data members to zero. The main function declares an array of two **Dates** and a single date with initialized values. It assigns the initialized **Date** to the first of the two **Dates** in the array and then displays both dates as follows:

```
6/24/40
0/0/0
```

Class Array Constructors

When you declare an array of objects of a class, the compiler calls the constructor function once for each element in the array. It is important that you understand this relationship when you design constructor functions.

Exercise 7-22 repeats Exercise 7-21, but it adds a display message to the constructor function to prove that the constructor gets called twice for one declaration.

```
#include <iostream.h>

// ------- date class
class Date {
    int mo, da, yr;
public:
    Date();
    Date(int m, int d, int y) { mo = m; da = d; yr = y;}
    void display()
        { cout << '\n' << mo << '/' << da << '/' <<yr; }
};


// constructor that is called for each element in a Date array
Date::Date()
{
    cout << "\nDate constructor running";
    mo = 0; da = 0; yr = 0;
}

main()
{
    Date dates[2];
    Date temp(6,24,40);

    dates[0] = temp;
    dates[0].display();
    dates[1].display();
}
```

Exercise 7-22 — Constructors for Arrays of Classes.

Exercise 7-22 displays the following messages:

```
Date constructor running
Date constructor running
6/24/40
0/0/0
```

As you can see, the constructor function executed twice, once for each of the elements in the array. There is no message displayed for the constructor of the **temp** object because it uses the constructor function that accepts initializers, which has no message.

Class Array Destructors

When an array of objects of a class goes out of scope, the compiler calls the destructor function once for each element of the array.

Exercise 7-23 illustrates calling destructors for class-array elements.

```
#include <iostream.h>

// ------- date class
class Date {
    int mo, da, yr;
public:
    Date() { mo = 0; da = 0; yr = 0; }
    Date(int m, int d, int y) { mo = m; da = d; yr = y;}
    ~Date();
    void display()
        { cout << '\n' << mo << '/' << da << '/' <<yr; }
};

// destructor that is called for each element in a Date array
Date::~Date()
{
    cout << "\nDate destructor running";
}

main()
{
    Date dates[2];
    Date temp(6,24,40);

    dates[0] = temp;
    dates[0].display();
    dates[1].display();
}
```

Exercise 7-23 — Destructors for Arrays of Classes.

This exercise copies Exercise 7-22, except that there is a destructor function which does nothing except display its execution on the console to prove that it runs more than once for an — array of objects. The following display shows that the destructor runs three times — twice for the two elements in the **dates** array and once for the **temp** object:

```
6/24/40
0/0/0
Date destructor running
Date destructor running
Date destructor running
```

Static Members

You can declare that a member of a class is **static**, in which case only one instance of it exists. It is accessible to all the member functions. No instance of the class needs to be declared for the static members to exist, although unless a static member is public, it cannot be seen by the rest of the program.

The declaration of a static member in a class does not automatically define the variable, however. You must define it outside of the class definition for it to exist. Versions of C++ earlier than 2.0 did not have this requirement.

> The Zortech C++ 2.1 compiler retained the earlier treatment of static class members in that they do not need to be defined outside of the class definition.

Static Data Members

You would use a static data member to maintain a global value that applies to all instances of the class. Member functions can modify this value, and all other objects of the class will then see the modified value. As an example, consider the simple linked list that Exercise 7-20 used. The class merely defined the list entries. It was up to the using program to keep track of the end of the list.

Exercise 7-24 improves the linked-list example in Exercise 7-20 with a static data member that holds the address of the last entry in the list.

```
#include <iostream.h>
#include <string.h>

class ListEntry {
    static ListEntry *lastentry; // static list head pointer
    char *listvalue;
    ListEntry *nextentry;
public:
    ListEntry();
    ListEntry(char *);
    ~ListEntry() { if (listvalue != NULL) delete listvalue;}
    ListEntry *NextEntry() { return nextentry; };
    void display() { cout << '\n' << listvalue; }
};

ListEntry *ListEntry::lastentry;

ListEntry::ListEntry()
{
    listvalue = NULL;
    nextentry = NULL;
    lastentry = this;
}

ListEntry::ListEntry(char *s)
{
    lastentry->nextentry = this;
    lastentry = this;
    listvalue = new char[strlen(s)+1];
    strcpy(listvalue, s);
    nextentry = NULL;
}
```

Exercise 7-24 continued...

…from previous page

```
   main()
   {
       ListEntry listhead;     // ---- this is the list head
       // ---------- read in some names
       while (1)    {
           cout << "\nEnter a name ('end' when done): ";
           char name[25];
           cin >> name;
           if (strncmp(name, "end", 3) == 0)
               break;
           // -------- make a list entry of the name
           new ListEntry(name);
       }
       ListEntry *next = listhead.NextEntry();
       // ------- display the names
       while (next != NULL)     {
           next->display();
           ListEntry *hold = next;
           next = next->NextEntry();
           // -------- delete the ListEntry
           delete hold;
       }
   }
```

Exercise 7-24 — Static Members and the Linked List.

Exercise 7-24 displays the following prompting messages. Enter names until you are done, then enter "end." The program displays the names in the order in which you entered them.

```
Enter a name ('end' when done): Fred
Enter a name ('end' when done): Joe
Enter a name ('end' when done): Al
Enter a name ('end' when done): Walter
Enter a name ('end' when done): Julian
Enter a name ('end' when done): end

Fred
Joe
Al
Walter
Julian
```

This exercise represents a much-improved linked-list class. By using a static data member to keep a record of the end of the list, the class assumes all the responsibility for list integrity. To use it, you must declare a class object with no initializers. The constructor for that form sets up a new list with a list entry as the list head. This constructor also initializes the static **lastentry** pointer to point to the list head entry. The **nextentry** pointer in that entry is initially NULL, but it will point to the first list entry that the program declares. That entry will point to the one following it, and subsequent entries will point to the ones following them. The last entry in the list will always have a NULL value in its **nextentry** pointer.

The constructor function for a list entry adds the entry to the list, so there is no need for the **AddEntry** function of Exercise 7-20. Observe that Exercise 7-24 uses the **new** operator to declare a new entry, and that it does not assign the address returned by the new operator to a pointer. Because the constructor function records the address of the entry in the **nextentry** pointer of the previous entry, the program does not need to otherwise remember the address.

Finally, the linked-list class defined in Exercise 7-24 allows the program to retrieve the entries in the same order in which they were added. After you enter all the names and type in the "end" input, the program displays those names in their original order, rather than in reverse order as did earlier versions of this program.

Static Member Functions

Member functions can be static as well. You can use static member functions to perform tasks in the name of the class or an object where the function does not need access to the members of any particular instance of the class. Usually you will use a static member function when you need to access only the static data members of a class.

Static member functions have no **this** pointer. Inasmuch as they have no access to the nonstatic members, they cannot use the **this** pointer to point to anything.

Exercise 7-25 adds a static member function to the **ListEntry** class. In this exercise, the function displays the last entry in the list, which is always the entry you just keyed in.

```
#include <iostream.h>
#include <string.h>

class ListEntry {
    static ListEntry *lastentry; // a static list head pointer
    char *listvalue;
    ListEntry *nextentry;
public:
    ListEntry();
    ListEntry(char *);
    ~ListEntry() { if (listvalue != NULL) delete listvalue; }
    ListEntry *NextEntry() { return nextentry; };
    void display() { cout << '\n' << listvalue; }
    // ------- a static member function
    static void showlast();
};

ListEntry *ListEntry::lastentry;

ListEntry::ListEntry()
{
    listvalue = NULL;
    nextentry = NULL;
    lastentry = this;
}
ListEntry::ListEntry(char *s)
{
    lastentry->nextentry = this;
    lastentry = this;
    listvalue = new char[strlen(s)+1];
    strcpy(listvalue, s);
    nextentry = NULL;
}

// ---------- a static member function
void ListEntry::showlast()
{
    lastentry->display();
    cout << " is the last entry in the list";
}
```

Exercise 7-25 continued...

...from previous page

```
main()
{
    ListEntry listhead;      // ---- this is the list head
    // ---------- read in some names
    while (1)    {
        cout << "\nEnter a name ('end' when done): ";
        char name[25];
        cin >> name;
        if (strncmp(name, "end", 3) == 0)
            break;
        // -------- make a list entry of the name
        new ListEntry(name);
        // ----- call the static member function
        listhead.showlast();
    }
    // ------- delete the entries
    ListEntry *next = listhead.NextEntry();
    while (next != NULL)     {
        ListEntry *hold = next;
        next = next->NextEntry();
        // -------- delete the ListEntry
        delete hold;
    }
}
```

Exercise 7-25 — Static Member Functions.

Exercise 7-25 displays the following prompting messages. Enter names until you are done, then enter "end." The program builds a linked list as you go and displays the last name in the list each time you enter a new one.

```
Enter a name ('end' when done): Alan
Alan is the last entry in the list
Enter a name ('end' when done): Sharon
Sharon is the last entry in the list
Enter a name ('end' when done): Wendy
Wendy is the last entry in the list
Enter a name ('end' when done): Tyler
Tyler is the last entry in the list
Enter a name ('end' when done): end
```

The **showlast** function is static. As such, it cannot read or write the member functions of the object for which it is called. But, because it needs to use the static **lastentry** pointer and nothing else, the function can be static, too.

Static Public Members

If a static member is public, it is accessible to the entire program and is not bound to a particular object. You can call a public static member function from anywhere without associating it with a particular instance of the class. The program in Exercise 7-25 called the **showlast** static member function in the name of the **listhead** object. In fact, the use of the object was for notational purposes only. Because the function is static, it could have been called in the name of any object. Further, because it is public, it can be called without an object reference at all. A public static-member function is not quite global. It exists only within the scope of the class in which it is defined. You can, however, call it from anywhere within that scope by prefixing it with the class name and using the **: :** scope resolution operator.

Exercise 7-26 modifies Exercise 7-25 to demonstrate how to call a public static member function without associating it with a particular object of the class.

```cpp
#include <iostream.h>
#include <string.h>

class ListEntry {
    static ListEntry *lastentry; // a static list head pointer
    char *listvalue;
    ListEntry *nextentry;
public:
    ListEntry();
    ListEntry(char *);
    ~ListEntry() { if (listvalue != NULL) delete listvalue; }
    ListEntry *NextEntry() { return nextentry; };
    void display() { cout << '\n' << listvalue; }
    // ------- a static member function
    static void showlast();
};

ListEntry *ListEntry::lastentry;

ListEntry::ListEntry()
{
    listvalue = NULL;
    nextentry = NULL;
    lastentry = this;
}
ListEntry::ListEntry(char *s)
{
    lastentry->nextentry = this;
    lastentry = this;
    listvalue = new char[strlen(s)+1];
    strcpy(listvalue, s);
    nextentry = NULL;
}
```

Exercise 7-26 continued...

…from previous page

```
// ---------- a static member function
void ListEntry::showlast()
{
    lastentry->display();
    cout << " is the last entry in the list";
}

main()
{
    ListEntry listhead;     // ---- this is the list head
    // ---------- read in some names
    while (1)    {
        cout << "\nEnter a name ('end' when done): ";
        char name[25];
        cin >> name;
        if (strncmp(name, "end", 3) == 0)
            break;
        // -------- make a list entry of the name
        new ListEntry(name);
        // ----- call the static member function
        // ----- with no object reference
        ListEntry::showlast();
    }
    // ------- delete the entries
    ListEntry *next = listhead.NextEntry();
    while (next != NULL)    {
        ListEntry *hold = next;
        next = next->NextEntry();
        // -------- delete the ListEntry
        delete hold;
    }
}
```

Exercise 7-26 — Public Static Member Functions.

Exercise 7-26 has the same displays and inputs as Exercise 7-25.

Public static members may be used when there is no instance of the class. Because they are both public and static, and you can call them in the name of the class alone, you can use one before you declare an object of the class.

Exercise 7-27 illustrates a class with a public static data member that the program initializes before declaring any objects of the class.

```cpp
#include <iostream.h>

class Date {
    int mo, da, yr;
public:
    static int format;    // 1 = mm/dd/yy, 2 = dd/mm/yy
    Date(int m , int d, int y) { mo = m; da = d; yr = y; }
    void display();
};

int Date::format;

void Date::display()
{
    if (format == 1)
        cout << mo << '/' << da;
    else
        cout << da << '/' << mo;
    cout << '/' << yr;
}
```

Exercise 7-27 continued...

...from previous page

```
main()
{
    char ch = '0';
    while (ch != '3')    {
        cout << "\n  1 = mm/dd/yy";
        cout << "\n  2 = dd/mm/yy";
        cout << "\n  3 = quit\n  ";
        cin >> ch;
        if (ch == '1' || ch == '2')    {
            Date::format = ch - '0'; // no Date declared yet
            // ---- declare and display a date
            Date dt(6, 24, 40);
            dt.display();
        }
    }
}
```

Exercise 7-27 — Using Public Static Members without Objects.

The **Date** class has a public static data member named **format** that controls whether the **display** member function displays the date in either the mm/dd/yy or the dd/mm/yy format. The program displays the following menu:

```
1 = mm/dd/yy
2 = dd/mm/yy
3 = quit
```

When you enter a 1 or a 2, the program initializes the **format** data member for the **Date** class even though no **Date** objects are in scope. Then, the program declares and displays the **dt** variable. One of the following two displays occurs, depending on what you typed into the menu:

```
6/24/40
24/6/40
```

Classes and the Free Store

In Chapter 3, you learned about the C++ free store and the **new** and **delete** memory-management operators. This section discusses those operators and their special relationship to class definitions.

Using `new` and `delete` to Manage Object Scope

An automatic class object usually comes into scope when it is declared and goes out of scope when the program exits the block in which the object is declared. You can override this behavior by using the **new** operator to construct an object. The object exists until you use the **delete** operator to destroy it. To use this feature, you must remember the address returned by **new** so that you can send it to **delete**. You must also remember the type of object that the pointer points to, because **delete** must know what type of object you are deleting. The type of object to be deleted is a function of the type of the pointer that you send to the **delete** operator.

Constructors and `new`, Destructors and `delete`

You used **new** and **delete** in earlier exercises to get and release memory for classes. When you use **new** to get memory for a class, the **new** operator function calls the class's constructor function. When you use **delete** to return the memory, the **delete** operator function calls the class's destructor function.

Exercise 7-28 illustrates the relationships between **new** and the constructor functions and **delete** and the destructor function.

```
#include <iostream.h>

class Date    {
    int mo, da, yr;
public:
    Date();
    ~Date();
};

Date::Date()
{
    cout << "\nDate constructor";
}

Date::~Date()
{
    cout << "\nDate destructor";
}

main()
{
    Date *dt = new Date;
    cout << "\nProcess the date";
    delete dt;
}
```

*Exercise 7-28 — **new** = Constructor, **delete** = Destructor.*

The exercise defines a **Date** class with a constructor and destructor. These functions simply display messages that say they are running. When the **new** operator initializes the **dt** pointer, the constructor function executes. When the **delete** operator deletes the memory pointed to by the pointer, it calls the destructor function.

Exercise 7-28 displays the following messages:

```
Date constructor
Process the date
Date destructor
```

The Free Store and Class Arrays

You learned earlier that constructor and destructor functions are called once for every element in an array of class objects.

Exercise 7-29 illustrates an incorrect way to delete arrays of new classes.

```
#include <iostream.h>

class Date    {
    int mo, da, yr;
public:
    Date()  { cout << "\nDate constructor"; }
    ~Date() { cout << "\nDate destructor";  }
};

main()
{
    Date *dt = new Date[5];
    cout << "\nProcess the dates";
    delete dt;                     // Not enough deletes!
}
```

*Exercise 7-29 — Deleting Arrays of **new** Classes.*

The **dt** pointer points to an array of five dates. The **Date** constructor function executes five times from the **new** operator because that is what the array notation tells the compiler to do. But the compiler has no indication from the call to **delete** that the pointer points to more than one **Date** object, so it builds only one call to the destructor function.

Exercise 7-29 displays the following messages:

```
Date constructor
Date constructor
Date constructor
Date constructor
Date constructor
Process the dates
Date destructor
```

To solve this problem, C++ allows you to tell the **delete** operator that the pointer being deleted points to an array. You do so with a subscript to the delete operator like this:

```
delete [number_of_elements] pointername;
```

C++ version 2.1 eliminates the requirement for the precise number of elements in the **delete** operator's bracketed parameter. You can achieve the correct result in C++ version 2.1 by coding **delete** this way:

```
delete [] pointername;
```

Because of this improvement to the way the **delete** operator works in C++ 2.1, programmers must be even more cautious about overloading the global **new** and **delete** operators in the manner described in Chapter 3. The **new** operator will need to remember the size and the number of elements in any array for which it provides memory so that the **delete** operator will know how many destructors to call and the array offsets to the address of the objects being destroyed.

Exercise 7-30 illustrates the correct use of the **delete** operator where an array is involved.

```
#include <iostream.h>

class Date    {
    int mo, da, yr;
public:
    Date()  { cout << "\nDate constructor"; }
    ~Date() { cout << "\nDate destructor";  }
};

main()
{
    Date *dt = new Date[5];
    cout << "\nProcess the dates";
    delete [5] dt;                      // deleting 5 items
}
```

*Exercise 7-30 — Correctly Deleting Arrays of **new** Classes.*

Exercise 7-30 displays the following messages:

```
Date constructor
Date constructor
Date constructor
Date constructor
Date constructor
Process the dates
Date destructor
Date destructor
Date destructor
Date destructor
Date destructor
```

If you pass a value to **delete** that is not the same as the number of elements in the array, you will get unpredictable results. If the value is less than the number of elements, the remaining elements will not be destroyed by your destructor, although their memory will be returned to the free store, and they will not be accessible to the program. If the value is greater, you will call the destructor with addresses of nonexistent objects and probably cause the program to crash, depending on what the destructor does.

If you use the array notation in the **delete** of an object that has no destructors, the compiler ignores the notation.

Overloaded Class `new` and `delete`

Chapter 3 taught you how to manage memory by writing overloaded **new** and **delete** operator functions. Those overloaded operators were for any use of **new** and **delete**. You can also overload **new** and **delete** from within the scope of a class definition. This feature allows a class to have its own custom **new** and **delete** operators. You will usually use this feature to gain some performance benefit from class-specific knowledge about the memory requirements of a class that can avoid the general-purpose overhead of the global **new** and **delete** operators.

Suppose that you know that there will never be more than a certain small number of instances of a class at any one time. You can allocate the necessary memory for all instances of that class and use class-specific **new** and **delete** operators to manage the memory.

Exercise 7-31 illustrates a class with overloaded **new** and **delete** operators that are specific to the class.

```cpp
#include <iostream.h>
#include <string.h>
#include <stddef.h>

const int MAXNAMES = 5;

class Names    {
    char name[25];
public:
    void setname(char *s) { strcpy(name, s); }
    void display() { cout << '\n' << name; }
    void *operator new(size_t);
    void operator delete(void *);
};

// -------- simple memory pool to handle fixed number of Names
char pool[MAXNAMES] [sizeof(Names)];
int inuse[MAXNAMES];

// -------- overloaded new operator for the Names class
void *Names::operator new(size_t)
{
    for (int p = 0; p < MAXNAMES; p++)
        if (!inuse[p])    {
            inuse[p] = 1;
            return pool+p;
        }
    return NULL;
}

// --------- overloaded delete operator for the Names class
void Names::operator delete(void *p)
{
    inuse[((char *)p - pool[0]) / sizeof(Names)] = 0;
}
```

Exercise 7-31 continued...

...from previous page

```
    main()
    {
        Names *nm[MAXNAMES];
        for (int i = 0; i < MAXNAMES; i++)    {
            cout << "\nEnter name # " << i+1 << ": ";
            char name[25];
            cin >> name;
            nm[i] = new Names;
            nm[i]->setname(name);
        }
        for (i = 0; i < MAXNAMES; i++)    {
            nm[i]->display();
            delete nm[i];
        }
    }
```

*Exercise 7-31 — Class-specific **new** and **delete** Operators.*

Exercise 7-31 prompts you for five names and then displays them as shown here:

```
Enter name # 1: Harpo
Enter name # 2: Chico
Enter name # 3: Groucho
Enter name # 4: Zeppo
Enter name # 5: Karl

Harpo
Chico
Groucho
Zeppo
Karl
```

A class of **Names** is defined in Exercise 7-31. The class has a member function that lets a user of the class set the name value of an object of the class. It also has a member function to display the name. Then it defines its own **new** and **delete** operators. Because the program is guaranteed never to exceed MAXNAMES names at one time, the programmer has decided to speed execution by overriding the default **new** and **delete** operators.

The simple memory pool that supports names is a **pool** character array with enough space to hold all the concurrent **Names** the program expects. The associated **inuse** integer array contains a true/false integer for each **Name** to indicate if an entry in the **pool** is in use.

The overloaded **new** operator finds an unused entry in the **pool** and returns its address. The overloaded **delete** operator marks the specified entry as unused.

Although a class design includes overloaded **new** and **delete** operators, the overloaded operator functions are not called for allocations of arrays of objects of the class. Suppose that the program in Exercise 7-31 included these statements:

```
Names *nms = new Names[10];
// ...
delete [10] nms;
```

These statements would call the global **new** and **delete** operators rather than the overloaded ones.

Overloaded **new** and **delete** functions within a class definition are always static and have no **this** pointer associated with the object being created or deleted. This is because the compiler calls the **new** function before it calls the class's constructor function, and it calls the **delete** function after it calls the destructor.

Exercise 7-32 demonstrates the sequence in which the constructor, destructor, and overloaded **new** and **delete** operator functions execute.

```
#include <iostream.h>

class Name    {
    char name[25];
public:
    Name()  { cout << "\nName constructor running"; }
    ~Name() { cout << "\nName destructor running";     }
    void *operator new(size_t);
    void operator delete(void *);
};

// -------- simple memory pool to handle one Name
char pool [sizeof(Name)];

// -------- overloaded new operator for the Name class
void *Name::operator new(size_t)
{
    cout << "\nName's new running";
    return pool;
}

// --------- overloaded delete operator for the Name class
void Name::operator delete(void *)
{
    cout << "\nName's delete running";
}

main()
{
    cout << "\nBuilding a new name";
    Name *nm = new Name;
    cout << "\nDeleting a name";
    delete nm;
}
```

*Exercise 7-32 — Class-specific **new** and **delete** Operators
with Constructor, Destructor.*

Exercise 7-32 does nothing with the class except display the following messages as the various functions execute:

```
Building a new name
Name's new running
Name constructor running
Deleting a name
Name destructor running
Name's delete running
```

As you can see, the **new** function executes before the constructor function. The **new** function may not access any of the class's members because no memory exists for them until **new** allocates it, and because the constructor function has not yet performed any other class-specific initializations. Likewise, because the **delete** operator executes after the destructor function, the **delete** operator may not have access to the class members.

Copy Constructors

A copy constructor is a class member function that executes when you initialize a new object of the class with an existing object of the same class. The copy constructor is similar to the conversion constructor function that you learned about earlier in this chapter. Conversion constructors convert the values in one class object to the format of an object of a different class. Copy constructors initialize the values from an existing object of a class to a new instantiated object of that same class.

Earlier in this chapter you learned how to overload the assignment operator (=) to manage the assignment of an object of a class to another object of the same class where the default bit-wise assignment provided by the compiler would cause problems. Similar problems occur when you initialize an object with the contents of another object, so you must have copy constructor functions.

The difference between initialization of an object with another object, and assignment of one object to another is this: assignment assigns the value of an existing object to another existing object; initialization creates a new object and initializes it with the contents of the existing object. The compiler can distinguish the two by using your overloaded assignment operator for assignments and your copy constructor for initializers. If you omit either one, the compiler will build a default bit-wise copy operation for the one you omit.

Initializing an object with the contents of another object of the same class requires the use of a copy constructor function, which is a constructor that can be called with a single argument of the same class as the object being constructed.

Exercise 7-33 demonstrates the copy constructor.

```
#include <iostream.h>
#include <string.h>

// ------- date class
class Date {
    int mo, da, yr;
    char *month;
public:
    Date(int m, int d, int y);
    Date(Date&);  // copy constructor
    ~Date();
    void display();
};

// constructor that is called for an initialized Date
Date::Date(int m, int d, int y)
{
    static char *mos[] = {
        "January", "February", "March", "April", "May",
        "June", "July", "August", "September", "October",
        "November", "December"
    };
    mo = m; da = d; yr = y;
    month = new char[strlen(mos[m-1])+1];
    strcpy(month, mos[m-1]);
}
```

Exercise 7-33 continued...

…from previous page

```
// ---------- Date copy constructor
Date::Date(Date& dt)
{
    mo = dt.mo;
    da = dt.da;
    yr = dt.yr;
    month = new char [strlen(dt.month)+1];
    strcpy(month, dt.month);
}

// Destructor for a Date
Date::~Date()
{
    if (month != NULL)
        delete month;
}

// ----------- display member function
void Date::display()
{
    if (month != NULL)
        cout << '\n' << month << ' ' << da << ", "
            << yr+1900;
}

main()
{
    // ------ first date
    Date birthday(6,24,40);
    birthday.display();
    // ------ second date
    Date newday = birthday;
    newday.display();
    // ------ third date
    Date lastday(birthday);
    lastday.display();
}
```

Exercise 7-33 — **Copy Constructor**.

The copy constructor in this exercise resembles the overloaded assignment operator in Exercise 7-18. The difference is that the copy constructor function executes when you declare a new **Date** object that is to be initialized with the contents of an existing **Date** object. The exercise shows that there are two ways to do this. One way uses the usual C++ variable initializer syntax as shown here.

```
Date newday = birthday;
```

The second way uses the constructor calling convention where the initializing object is an argument to the function's parameter as shown here:

```
Date lastday(birthday);
```

The Management of Class Source and Object Files

In all the previous exercises, each program has been a single, stand-alone source module. The entire program was contained in one source module that represented the exercise. In actual practice, you will not organize a C++ source program that way. You will use the traditional C convention of having common definitions in header files, common executable code in separately compiled object libraries, and separately compiled source code files for the code that supports your application.

Class Definitions in a Header

The convention for C++ header files resembles that of C. Put things in header files that do not reserve memory but that define structures, classes, and externally defined items to the source modules that include header files. Where a class uses the definitions of other classes, its **include** file will include those of the other classes. This opens the possibility for multiple or circular inclusions. You should use a code convention that prevents the errors that could occur if a source file is included twice or if source file A includes source file B which includes source file C which includes source file A.

If you have a class named **Date**, for example, you might put its definition in a header file named *date.h*. If you use the **#ifndef** preprocessor directive shown in the following listing, you can prevent those cases where a header file might be included more than once or where header file inclusion wraps around:

```
#ifndef DATE_H
#define DATE_H
// --- the contents of date.h
#endif
```

Class Member Functions in a Library

As a general rule, you should separately compile the member functions of your classes and maintain them as separate object files, perhaps in object library files. The source files for the member functions will, of course, include the header files that define the classes to which the functions belong, as well as those for any classes that they may use and that might not be included from within the class header.

Summary

This chapter taught you about C++ classes. Chapter 8 is about overloaded operators, a feature that you touched on here and in Chapter 3. In Chapter 3, you learned to overload the **new** and **delete** operators to insert your own memory-management functions into the program. In this chapter you learned the same technique, but at the individual class level. You also learned to overload the assignment operator to build conversion functions and to manage class copying where a binary or member-by-member copy would not work.

The potential for overloaded operators extends beyond the uses you've learned so far. With them you can perform arithmetic, comparisons, and many other operations on your classes just as if they were standard C++ data types. Chapter 8 describes these features.

Chapter 8

Overloaded Operators

This chapter is about how you can extend the C++ language by adding operators to your classes. When you design a class, you add a new data type to the C++ language. You have already learned how you can add dates and other such types by binding data structures to the functions that manipulate them. Now you will learn how to add operators to those classes.

Suppose that you designed a numerical type and wanted to logically add some number of them together to arrive at a logical sum. Also, suppose you wanted to compare two of your new data types. You could build special class member functions to perform these operations and call them in the manner that you call the standard C function **strcmp**, for example. There is a better way.

The C++ language includes a feature that lets you build operators that implement unary and binary operations on objects of classes. The feature is called *operator overloading*, and with it you write special member functions that implement the overloaded operators on your classes.

In Chapters 3 and 7 you overloaded the **new** and **delete** operators to build custom memory management into your classes and the program at large. You also overloaded the assignment operator in Chapter 7 to build conversion and copy functions for your classes.

Perhaps without realizing it, you have already used overloaded operators extensively in most of the exercises in all the chapters. Every time you sent a display value to the **cout** object, you used the << bit-wise shift left operator as overloaded by the standard output stream class.

Overloading an operator means that you write a function to make the operator do your bidding. For example, you can build code that lets you do this with a **Date** class:

```
Date dt(1,2,83);
dt += 100;
```

(The **Date** class appeared in many of the examples in Chapter 7.) You can overload an operator to make it work in a special way with a class within the boundaries of some rules:

1. You cannot use an operator in a way that is not permitted by the syntax of the compiler. For example, you cannot do the following in C++:

    ```
    int a;
    / a;
    ```

    Therefore, you cannot overload the / operator to do the following either:

    ```
    Date dt(1,2,83);
    / dt;
    ```

2. This rule is a syntactical one. If you can put an operator between two identifiers, then you can overload it for custom use with your classes, even if the operator would not be otherwise acceptable to the compiler. Consider the following statement:

    ```
    cout << "Hello";
    ```

Without an overloaded << operator, that expression would have tried to shift **cout** a number of bits equal to the value of the pointer to the string. None of that would have gotten past the compiler. But the statement is syntactically, if not grammatically, correct so you can write an overloaded operator function that will execute when this construct appears.

3. You cannot overload the way an operator works with the C++ fixed data types. For example, you cannot rewrite the addition operator between two integers to make it perform differently.

4. You cannot invent new operators that do not exist in the C++ language. For example, you cannot devise your own operator.

5. You cannot overload certain operators. The following operators are not available to be overloaded:

Operator	Definition
.	Class member operator
. *	Pointer-to-member operator
: :	Scope resolution operator
? :	Conditional expression operator

As you learn and apply these techniques try to keep a rein on your enthusiasm for their use. You can easily get carried away with overloaded operators to the extent that your code becomes difficult to understand. If you load up your classes with lots of overloaded operators, other programmers will need to constantly refer back to the overloaded operator functions to see what they do. If the code is in libraries, it might not be available for review. You might even find yourself in the same circumstance if enough time has passed since you originally wrote the code. At the very least, use liberal comments in the class definition header files to document the behavior of the operators you overload.

Binary Arithmetic Operators

Consider this example. You have a **Date** class such as the one that you used in the exercises in Chapter 7. Your system requires that you derive a new date by adding an integer number of days to the date. Rather than calling a function to make the addition, you prefer to use the following syntax in the code that does the addition:

```
Date newdate = olddate + 100;
```

Assuming that **olddate** was an object of type **Date** with a value already in it, the result would be a **newdate** object of type **Date** that had the correct month, day, and year adjusted by 100 days.

Class Member Operator Functions

To make your class work in arithmetic addition expressions, you would write a function that overloads the + operator when it appears between a **Date** object and an integer. For this example, you will build the overloaded operator into the class definition.

Exercise 8-1 demonstrates how to overload the + operator to perform integer addition on the **Date** class.

```
#include <iostream.h>

class Date {
    int mo, da, yr;
public:
    Date() {}
    Date(int m, int d, int y) { mo = m; da = d; yr = y; }
    void display() { cout << mo << '/' << da << '/' << yr; }
    Date operator+(int);        // overloaded + operator
};

static int dys[] = {31,28,31,30,31,30,31,31,30,31,30,31};
// -------- overloaded + operator
Date Date::operator+(int n)
{
    Date dt = *this;
    n += dt.da;
    while (n > dys[dt.mo-1])    {
        n -= dys[dt.mo-1];
        if (++dt.mo == 13)    {
            dt.mo = 1;
            dt.yr++;
        }
    }
    dt.da = n;
    return dt;
}

main()
{
    Date olddate(2,20,90);
    Date newdate;
    newdate = olddate + 21;    // three weeks hence
    newdate.display();
}
```

Exercise 8-1 — Overloading the + Operator.

Exercise 8-1 displays the following date.

3/13/90

Nonmember Operator Functions

In Exercise 8-1, the + operator is overloaded by using a member function. Overloaded operator member functions have an implied first argument that is the object for which the operator executes. In this case, the argument is the **olddate** object taken from the left side of the binary expression. Because of this behavior, the left argument of a member operator functions must be an object of the class. But suppose you wanted to support the following expression as well:

```
Date newdate = 100 + olddate;
```

This technique will not work, and there is no way to design a member operator function to do it. You can, however, provide a **friend** function that overloads an operator in this way.

Exercise 8-2 adds a **friend** function to the program in Exercise 8-1 to overload the + operator.

```
#include <iostream.h>

class Date {
    int mo, da, yr;
public:
    Date() {}
    Date(int m, int d, int y) { mo = m; da = d; yr = y; }
    void display() { cout << mo << '/' << da << '/' << yr; }
    // ----- overloaded + operators
    Date operator+(int);
    friend Date operator+(int n, Date& dt) { return dt + n;}
};
```

Exercise 8-2 continued...

...from previous page

```
static int dys[] = {31,28,31,30,31,30,31,31,30,31,30,31};
// -------- overloaded + operator
Date Date::operator+(int n)
{
    Date dt = *this;
    n += dt.da;
    while (n > dys[dt.mo-1])    {
        n -= dys[dt.mo-1];
        if (++dt.mo == 13)    {
            dt.mo = 1;
            dt.yr++;
        }
    }
    dt.da = n;
    return dt;
}

main()
{
    Date olddate(2,20,90);
    Date newdate;
    newdate = 21 + olddate;    // three weeks hence
    newdate.display();
}
```

Exercise 8-2 — Overloading the + Operator with a **Friend**.

Exercise 8-2 displays the same output as Exercise 8-1.

The **friend** function that overloads the + operator to allow addition with the arguments reversed simply calls the earlier one with the arguments turned around. Because the function is so small, it is an **inline** function.

Operator functions such as the **friend** function in Exercise 8-2 have both parameters declared, rather than using the implied parameter of the member operator function. Incidentally, you could write the first overloaded + function as a **friend** function as well. Many programmers overload all their class operators as **friend** functions for consistency.

There is nothing about the use of the addition operator that says the operator function must do addition. The overloaded operator function will do whatever you design it to do. You use operator functions as a way to get the compiler to call your code when it sees the operator applied to the object in the syntax that corresponds to the parameter types of the function.

> You might have guessed by now that you could overload the addition operator to perform subtraction. Yes, you could, but it would not be a wise thing to do.

The examples just given deal with addition. You can use the same approaches to develop overloaded subtraction, multiplication, division, modulus, Boolean, and shifting operator functions. Once again, nothing requires you to make those functions perform the operations implied by the operators. As a general rule, however, you should use operators to perform operations similar to their regular use in the C++ language.

Relational Operators

Suppose you want to compare dates. Perhaps you need to use an expression such as the following one:

```
if (newdate < olddate)
// ....
```

You can overload relational operators by using the same approaches that overloaded the addition operator in the preceding exercises.

Exercise 8-3 shows the **Date** class with overloaded operators that compare dates.

```
#include <iostream.h>

class Date {
    int mo, da, yr;
public:
    Date(int m, int d, int y) { mo = m; da = d; yr = y; }
    void display() { cout << mo << '/' << da << '/' << yr; }
    // ----- overloaded operators
    int operator==(Date& dt)
     { return this->mo==dt.mo &&
        this->da==dt.da && this->yr==dt.yr;}
    int operator<(Date&);
};
int Date::operator<(Date& dt)
{
    if (this->yr == dt.yr)    {
        if (this->mo == dt.mo)
            return this->da < dt.da;
        return this->mo < dt.mo;
    }
    return this->yr < dt.yr;
}
main()
{
    Date date1(12,7,41), date2(2,22,90), date3(12,7,41);

    if (date1 < date2)    {
        date1.display();
        cout << " is less than ";
        date2.display();
    }
    cout << '\n';
    if (date1 == date3)    {
        date1.display();
        cout << " is equal to ";
        date3.display();
    }
}
```

Exercise 8-3 — Overloading Relational Operators.

The **Date** class in Exercise 8-3 has two overloaded relational operators, the == (equal to) and the < (less than) operators. The main function declares three dates and compares them, displaying the following messages to demonstrate the effects of the comparisons:

```
12/7/41 is less than 2/22/90
12/7/41 is equal to 12/7/41
```

You could easily build the other relational operators as variations on the two that the exercise has. For example, the != (not equal) operator could be coded the following way:

```
int operator!=(Date& dt) { return !(*this == dt); }
```

Assignment Operators

You already learned how to overload assignment operators in the discussion on conversion and assignment functions in Chapter 7. C++ and C have the += and −= forms of assignment operators where the assignment includes an arithmetic, Boolean, or shift operation that is applied to the receiving field. You can overload these operators to work with your classes.

Exercise 8-4 adds the overloaded += operator to the **Date** class by using the overloaded + operator that the class already has.

```
#include <iostream.h>

class Date {
    int mo, da, yr;
public:
    Date() {}
    Date(int m, int d, int y) { mo = m; da = d; yr = y; }
    void display() { cout << mo << '/' << da << '/' << yr; }
    Date operator+(int);       // overloaded + operator
      // --------- overloaded += operator
    Date operator+=(int n) { *this = *this + n; return *this; }
};
```

Exercise 8-4 continued...

...from previous page

```
static int dys[] = {31,28,31,30,31,30,31,31,30,31,30,31};
// -------- overloaded + operator
Date Date::operator+(int n)
{
    Date dt = *this;
    n += dt.da;
    while (n > dys[dt.mo-1])    {
        n -= dys[dt.mo-1];
        if (++dt.mo == 13)     {
            dt.mo = 1;
            dt.yr++;
        }
    }
    dt.da = n;
    return dt;
}

main()
{
    Date olddate(2,20,90);
    olddate += 21;              // three weeks hence
    olddate.display();
}
```

Exercise 8-4 — Overloading the += Operator.

Exercise 8-4 displays the same output as Exercises 8-1 and 8-2.

Auto-increment and Auto-decrement

You can overload the ++ (auto-increment) and the −− (auto-decrement) operators within your classes, but, unless you are using C++ 2.1, the operator functions will not be able to tell whether these operators are prefix or postfix.

Exercise 8-5 adds the overloaded ++ operator to the **Date** class by using the overloaded + operator that the class already has.

```
#include <iostream.h>

class Date {
    int mo, da, yr;
public:
    Date() {}
    Date(int m, int d, int y) { mo = m; da = d; yr = y; }
    void display()
        { cout << '\n' << mo << '/' << da << '/' << yr;}
    Date operator+(int);        // overloaded +
      // --------- overloaded prefix ++ operator
    Date operator++() { *this = *this + 1; return *this; }
      // --------- overloaded C++ 2.1 postfix ++ operator
    // Remove the following function if you are using
    // C++ 2.0 or some versions of CFRONT 2.1 (see text)
    Date operator++(int)
      { Date dt = *this; *this = *this + 1; return dt; }
};
```

Exercise 8-5 continued...

…from previous page

```
static int dys[] = {31,28,31,30,31,30,31,31,30,31,30,31};
// -------- overloaded + operator
Date Date::operator+(int n)
{
    Date dt = *this;
    n += dt.da;
    while (n > dys[dt.mo-1])     {
        n -= dys[dt.mo-1];
        if (++dt.mo == 13)     {
            dt.mo = 1;
            dt.yr++;
        }
    }
    dt.da = n;
    return dt;
}

main()
{
    Date olddate(2,20,90);
    olddate++;
    olddate.display();
    ++olddate;
    olddate.display();
}
```

Exercise 8-5 — Overloading the ++ Operator.

Exercise 8-5 displays these dates.

```
2/21/90
2/22/90
```

In C++ 2.0, because both the prefix and postfix forms of the ++ operator cause the compiler to call the overloaded ++ operator function, there is no way for the function to know whether to return the value of the date before or after the increment. The exercise returns the value after the increment. Which value you would return would depend on how you chose to use the operator. Obviously, this is a case where the behavior of the overload cannot exactly emulate that of the compiler's regular use of the operator. For this reason, you should hesitate before using it to increment the values in a class object. Its use could compromise the readability of your code.

In C++ Version 2.1, you can specify that the auto-increment and auto-decrement operators are prefix or postfix. The technique you learned in Exercise 8-5 for overloading the ++ operator defines a prefix auto-increment operator in C++ Version 2.1. To define a postfix auto-increment operator, Exercise 8-5 would uses the following public member function in the class definition:

```
Date operator++(int)
```

The presence of the unnamed **int** variable in the function declaration tells the 2.1 compiler to call this function when it sees the postfix ++ operator. The code in the function must, of course, do what is required to support the postfix operation. In the case of the example above, the overloaded **operator++(int)** function saves the value of the object being incremented before it calls the overloaded **operator+( )** function to add one to it. After the addition, the saved object is returned.

> The TopSpeed C++ 2.1 compiler implements the postfix and prefix overloaded ++ and -- operators. The Comeau C++ 2.1 does not, because, at the time this is being written, AT&T has not released a version 2.1 of CFRONT that implements the new convention. The AT&T Reference Manual and the Annotated Reference Manual (see the bibliography) both define the convention, however.

Address-of and Reference-to Operator

You can overload the **&** (address-of) operator with the same qualification. The overloaded operator function will not know whether the notation was prefix or postfix unless the function declaration includes other parameters for the compiler to match.

One use for the overloaded **&** operator is to take the address of one of the data members, usually the most significant one, to pass to a library function that expects an address.

Exercise 8-6 demonstrates overloading the **&** operator.

```
#include <iostream.h>
#include <string.h>

class Name {
    char name[25];
public:
    void display() { cout << '\n' << name; }
    char * operator&() { return this->name; }
};

main()
{
    Name names[5];
    for (int i = 0; i < 5; i++)     {
        cout << "\nEnter a name: ";
        cin >> &names[i];
    }
    for (i = 0; i < 5; i++)
        cout << '\n' << &names[i];
}
```

*Exercise 8-6 — Overloaded **&** Operator.*

In Exercise 8-6, you enter five names in response to the prompt. The program then displays the names in the order in which you entered them:

```
Enter a name: John
Enter a name: Bill
Enter a name: Terry
Enter a name: Warren
Enter a name: Lou

John
Bill
Terry
Warren
Lou
```

The exercise overloads the **&** operator to return the address of the **name** array from within the class. The input from **cin** goes to that address. Because the **cin** object is an object of a class that will accept a character pointer along with its **own** overloaded **<<** operator, the return value from the overloaded **&** operator in the **Date** class works. Similarly, the output to **cout** is the same address.

> Note that if you overload the **&** operator this way to take the address of one of an object's data members, you can no longer use the operator to take the address of the object itself. If you need to be able to take the address of the object as well, you should use a regular member function to return the address of the data member of an object and let the **&** operator perform its normal function.

Unary Plus and Minus Operators

You can overload the unary plus and minus operators to work with a class. Suppose you have a class that describes an inventory quantity and you need to express that quantity with the plus and minus unary operators.

Exercise 8-7 is an example of how overloading the unary minus operator might work.

```
#include <iostream.h>
#include <string.h>

class ItemQty {
    int onhand;
    char desc[25];
public:
    ItemQty(int oh, char *d) { onhand = oh; strcpy(desc, d); }
    void display() { cout << '\n' << desc << ": " << onhand; }
    // ---- overloaded unary - operator
    int operator-() { return -onhand; }
};

main()
{
    ItemQty item1(100, "crankshaft");
    ItemQty item2(-50, "driveshaft");
    item1.display();
    cout << '\n' << -item1;        // invoke the overloaded -
    item2.display();
    cout << '\n' << -item2;        // invoke the overloaded -
}
```

Exercise 8-7 — Overloaded Unary Minus.

The exercise declares two **ItemQty** objects, one with a positive **onhand** value and one with a negative. It calls the **display** function to display the record contents and then uses the overloaded unary minus operator to display the quantity with the unary minus operator applied, as shown in the following display:

```
crankshaft: 100
-100
driveshaft: -50
50
```

Subscript Operator

There are times when overloading the [ ] (subscript) operator makes sense. For example, suppose you had a **String** class that stored a string value. You might want subscripted access to the character positions of the string value.

Exercise 8-8 is an example of an overloaded [ ] operator.

```
#include <iostream.h>
#include <string.h>

class String     {
    char *sptr;
public:
    String(char *);
    ~String() { delete sptr; }
    void display() { cout << '\n' << sptr; }
    char& operator[] (int n) { return *(sptr + n); }
};

String::String(char *s)
{
    sptr = new char[strlen(s)+1];
    strcpy(sptr, s);
}

main()
{
    String mystring("The Ides of March");
    mystring.display();
    cout << '\n' << mystring[4];
    mystring[4] = '1';
    mystring[5] = '5';
    mystring[6] = 't';
    mystring[7] = 'h';
    mystring.display();
    strncpy(&mystring[4], "21st", 4);
    mystring.display();
}
```

Exercise 8-8 — Overloaded [ ] *Operator.*

The exercise declares a string with a value. The overloaded [ ] operator function allows the program to retrieve a single character from the string and display it. Because the [ ] operator function returns a reference to the character being subscripted, the program can use the expression on the left side of an assignment. With that notation, the program inserts the value 15th one character at a time into the string and displays it. Then, by using the address of the value returned, the program uses **strncpy** to insert the value 21st into the string and displays it.

Exercise 8-8 displays the following messages when you run it:

```
The Ides of March
I
The 15th of March
The 21st of March
```

Note that the overloaded [ ] subscript operator may only be a nonstatic member function. You cannot implement it as a **friend** function in the manner of other operators.

Suppose you wanted to complete the similarity between your string classes and the character arrays of C++, where the following expressions are equivalent:

```
mystring[5]
*(mystring+5)
```

The following expressions are also equivalent:

```
&mystring[5]
mystring+5;
```

Exercise 8-9 shows how the overloaded + operator can simulate dereferenced pointer notation in a string class.

```cpp
#include <iostream.h>
#include <string.h>

class String    {
    char *sptr;
public:
    String(char *);
    ~String() { delete sptr; }
    void display() { cout << '\n' << sptr; }
    char& operator[] (int n) { return *(sptr + n); }
    char *operator+  (int n) { return sptr + n; }
};

String::String(char *s)
{
    sptr = new char[strlen(s)+1];
    strcpy(sptr, s);
}

main()
{
    String mystring("The Ides of March");
    mystring.display();
    cout << '\n' << *(mystring+4);
    *(mystring+4) = '1';
    *(mystring+5) = '5';
    *(mystring+6) = 't';
    *(mystring+7) = 'h';
    mystring.display();
    strncpy(mystring+4, "21st", 4);
    mystring.display();
}
```

Exercise 8-9 — Overloaded + Operator.

The exercise adds the overloaded + operator and changes its annotation from subscripted array accesses of the string to dereferenced pointer accesses. Other than for those differences, Exercise 8-9 is the same as Exercise 8-8.

Function Call Operator

When you overload the ( ) function call operator, you create a notation that makes your object's name look like a function that accepts whatever arguments you specify. You can, therefore, use the format to send many different message types to the object in the true spirit of object-oriented programming.

How you will use the overloaded ( ) function call operator will depend on your class and your imagination.

Exercise 8-10 illustrates one possibility for using the overloaded ( ) operator.

```
#include <iostream.h>
#include <string.h>

class Name {
    char name[25];
public:
    Name(char *s) { strcpy(name, s); }
    void operator() (char *s) { strcpy(s, name); }
};

main()
{
    Name nm("Charlie");
    char newname[25];
    nm(newname);          // use overloaded () to get name value
    cout << newname;
}
```

Exercise 8-10 — Overloaded ( ) Operator.

Exercise 8-10 displays the name "Charlie" on the screen.

The exercise uses the overloaded ( ) operator with a **char** pointer as an argument to deliver the contents of the **Name** class to the caller. You can use several different versions of the overloaded ( ) operator as long as each one has a distinct parameter list.

Note that the overloaded ( ) function call operator may only be a nonstatic member function. You cannot implement it as a **friend** function in the manner of other operators.

Pointer-to-member Operator

The –> operator, when overloaded, is always a unary operator with the class object (or reference to same) on its left. The function must return either the address of a class object or an object that itself has the –> operator overloaded.

You can overload the –> operator to assure that a pointer to a class object always has a value. Rather than declaring a simple pointer and always testing it for NULL, you can build a smart pointer to an object. The pointer always guarantees that it points to something meaningful, and you avoid the NULL pointer problems that plague programmers who neglect to test pointers before they use them.

Exercise 8-11 uses the usual **Date** class and, at the beginning of the program, a pointer to an object of the **Date** class.

```
#include <iostream.h>

class Date {
    int mo, da, yr;
public:
    Date(int m, int d, int y) { mo = m; da = d; yr = y; }
    void display()
        { cout << '\n' << mo << '/' << da << '/' << yr; }
};

main()
{
    Date *dp;              // a date pointer with garbage in it
    Date dt(3,17,90);      // a Date
    dp = &dt;              // put address of date in pointer
    dp->display();         // display date through the pointer
}
```

Exercise 8-11 — Pointer to Class Object.

Exercise 8-11 displays the date 3/17/90 on the screen.

The program declares a **Date** object, puts its address in the pointer, and calls the **display** member function through the pointer. Nothing is wrong with that. However, if the programmer neglects to assign a valid address of a **Date** object to the pointer, the program crashes because the pointer points nowhere meaningful. Whatever gets executed by that function call is not likely to be a valid function.

Exercise 8-12 adds a so-called smart pointer to the program.

```cpp
#include <iostream.h>

class Date {
    int mo, da, yr;
public:
    Date(int m, int d, int y) { mo = m; da = d; yr = y; }
    void display()
        { cout << '\n' << mo << '/' << da << '/' << yr; }
};
// ----------- "smart" Date pointer
class DatePtr {
    static Date *dp;
public:
    DatePtr() {}
    DatePtr(Date *d) { dp = d; }
    Date *operator->();
};

Date *DatePtr::dp;

Date *DatePtr::operator->()
{
    static Date nulldate(0,0,0);
    if (dp == NULL)         // if the pointer is NULL
        return &nulldate;   // return the dummy address
    return dp;              // otherwise return the pointer
}


main()
{
    DatePtr dp;             // a date pointer with nothing in it
    dp->display();          // use it to call display function
    Date dt(3,17,90);       // a Date
    dp = &dt;               // put address of date in pointer
    dp->display();          // display date through the pointer
}
```

Exercise 8-12 — Overloaded –> Operator.

Exercise 8-12 displays an empty date and a real one as shown here.

```
0/0/0
3/17/90
```

An object of the **DatePtr** class is a pointer that knows whether or not a value has ever been assigned to it. If the program tries to use the pointer without first assigning the address of a **Date** object to it, the pointer contains the address of a null **Date** instead of garbage. The **DatePtr** object will always return the address of a **Date** object or the address of the null **Date** because the **DatePtr** constructor conversion function accepts no value that is not the address of a **Date**.

Note that the overloaded –> pointer operator may only be a nonstatic member function. You cannot implement it as a **friend** function in the manner of other operators.

Summary

This chapter showed you how to overload C++ operators to work with your classes. Chapter 9 shows how you use the class inheritance features of C++ to derive new classes from old ones.

Chapter 9

Class Inheritance

C lass inheritance is the technique used to build new classes from old ones and to build object-oriented class hierarchies. You can build several layers of classes that are derived from other classes. You can build a network of classes by using the features of multiple inheritance. This chapter describes these processes by using small classes with easy-to-understand exercises.

Base and Derived Classes

You can derive a new class from any class that is available to your program. The class from which you derive is called the *base* class and the new class is called the *derived* class. A derived class can be a base class to a lower derived class as well.

One base class can have many derived classes, which in turn can have derived classes of its own, forming a class hierarchy.

With multiple inheritance, one derived class can have many base classes, each of which can have base classes of its own. This forms a class network.

When you derive a class, the new class inherits all the characteristics of its base. The derived class automatically possesses the data members and member functions of the base. The derived class can add its own members, but the base members become part of the derived class. Adding derived class members is how you modify the behavior of a base to form a derived class.

There are two reasons to derive a class. One is that you want to modify the behavior of an existing class. The other is that you are building a well-organized, object-oriented class hierarchy where your user-defined data types descend from one root class. These two reasons are design approaches, but the class inheritance behavior of C++ that supports them is the same, with the same rules and boundaries, regardless of your reason.

Why use inheritance to modify the behavior of an existing class? Why not just dig out the code and change the base class, making it do what you want it to do? There are several reasons.

First, the base class might be in use by other parts of your program, and you want its original behavior to remain intact for those objects that already use it. By deriving a class from the base, you define a new data type that inherits all the qualities of the base without disturbing its purpose to the rest of the program.

Second, the source code for the base class might not be available to you. The minimum resources that you need to use a defined class are its definition and the object code for its member functions. If you are using class libraries from other sources, you might not have the source code for the member functions.

Third, the base class might be defined as an abstract data type, which is a class that is designed to be a base. A class hierarchy contains general-purpose classes that do nothing themselves. Their purpose is to define the behavior of some generic data structure to which derived classes add the implementation details. Such base classes are known as abstract data types. An abstract list class, for example, can define the methods that manage the inserting, changing deleting, reordering, and searching of entries in the list without defining any actual entry values. Until you derive a class that describes the data in the list, the list class does nothing.

Fourth, your purpose in building a class hierarchy is to derive the benefits of the object-oriented approach. One of these benefits is the ability to use general-purpose class methods that modify their own behavior based on the characteristics of the subclasses that use them. The class hierarchy approach supports this ability through the virtual function mechanism. You will learn about this technique later in the chapter.

Simple Inheritance

You have been dealing with base classes since Chapter 5. All C++ structures and classes can have derived classes. You do not define the inheritance from within the base class, you do it from within the derived class. The base class has nothing in it that tells it what classes derive from it.

> Every exercise in this book up to this point has been an independent, stand-alone program. Now, you will begin to define some things in header files and link the object code of multiple source files to make running programs.

Exercise 9-1 is a header file named *timeday.h*. It contains the definition of a **Time** class, and it is similar to the class definitions that you learned in Chapter 7.

```
// ---------- timeday.h

#ifndef TIMEDAY_H
#define TIMEDAY_H

#include <iostream.h>
//
// A Time Class
//
class Time    {
    int hours, minutes, seconds;
public:
    Time(int hr, int min, int sec)
        { hours = hr; minutes = min; seconds = sec; }
    void display()
        { cout << hours << ':' << minutes << ':' << seconds; }
};

#endif
```

Exercise 9-1 — Header File to Define the **Time** *Class.*

The class in Exercise 9-1 is self-contained. All its member functions are **inline**. If the class had member functions that were not **inline**, their source code would appear in another source file that would include *timeday.h*, which you would compile independently to link with your program.

You do not compile or execute Exercise 9-1 by itself. It is a header file to be included in later exercises.

Designing a Derived Class

You haven't used the **Time** class for anything yet. Perhaps other programs use it regularly. Looking at it, you decide that while you need its basic properties for storing the time of day, your program needs to record and report the time zone as well as the hours, minutes, and seconds that the **Time** class supports. You can't simply modify the **Time** class because that would disturb the other programs that use it. You can, however, derive a class from it that adds the new requirements.

Exercise 9-2 is *timezone.h*, a header file that defines the **TimeZone** class, a class that maintains and displays the time along with its time zone. Like Exercise 9-1, Exercise 9-2 is a header file that you will include in the next exercise.

```
// ---------- timezone.h

#ifndef TIMEZONE_H
#define TIMEZONE_H

#include "timeday.h"
//
// A TimeZone Class
//

enum timezone { gmt, est, cst, mst, pst };
char *TZ[] = { "GMT", "EST", "CST", "MST", "PST" };

class TimeZone : public Time {
protected:
    timezone zone;
public:
    TimeZone(int hr, int min, int sec, timezone zn)
            : Time(hr, min, sec)
        { zone = zn; }
    void display()
        { Time::display(); cout << ' ' << TZ [zone]; }
};

#endif
```

Exercise 9-2 — Header to Define Derived **TimeZone** *Class.*

The **TimeZone** class is derived from the base class **Time**. You specify a base class with the **:** operator following the derived class name, as illustrated in the following statement:

```
class TimeZone : Time { /* ... */ };
```

> The declaration of the TZ array of character pointers in Exercise 9-2 violates the convention that says that header files should not declare anything that reserves memory. This lapse in discipline is to keep the exercise short and the class self-contained in one source file. In practice, most class definitions will require two source files, one for the definitions and one for the non-inline member functions and external data items, and the TZ array would be in that second source file.

Protected Members

The one difference between the **TimeZone** class in Exercise 9-2 and the ones you have used so far is the **protected** access specifier that appears ahead of the data member. You learned about **public** and **private** members in Chapter 7. Protected members are just like private members until a new class is derived from a base class that has protected members.

If a base class has private members, those members are not accessible to the derived class. Protected members are public to derived classes but private to the rest of the program. Use of the **protected** keyword is the only acknowledgment by the **TimeZone** class in *timezone.h* that it might ever be a base class.

When you design a class, you should proceed as if the class would someday be derived, even if you have no such intentions. Specify the **protected** keyword for members that could be accessible to derived classes.

The **TimeZone** class has one protected data member, the **zone** variable. It also has, indirectly, three other data members. These are the three private data members of the **Time** class: **hours**, **minutes**, and **seconds**. But because these members are private to the **Time** class, the member functions of the **TimeZone** class cannot have access to them except through the public member functions of the **Time** class.

Public and Private Base Classes

A derived class can specify that a base class is public or private by using the following notation in the definition of the derived class:

```
class TimeZone : private Time { /* ... */ };
class DispTime : public Time  { /* ... */ };
```

The **private** access specifier means that the protected and public members of the base class are private members of the derived class. The **public** access specifier means that the protected members of the base class are protected members of the derived class and the public members of the base class are public members of the derived class.

If you do not provide an access specifier, the compiler assumes that it will be private unless the base class is a structure, in which case the compiler assumes public.

Constructors in the Base and Derived Classes

When you declare an object of a derived class, the compiler executes the constructor function of the base class followed by the constructor function of the derived class.

The parameter list for the derived class's constructor function could be different from that of the base class's constructor function. Therefore, the constructor function for the derived class must tell the compiler what values to use as arguments to the constructor function for the base class.

The declaration of the derived class's constructor function specifies the arguments to the base class's constructor function as follows:

```
TimeZone(int hr, int min, int sec, timezone zn)
        : Time(hr, min, sec)
```

The : operator after the derived constructor's parameter list specifies that an argument list for a base class's constructor follows. The argument list is in parentheses and follows the name of the base class.

Note that the base constructor arguments appear in the declaration rather than in the definition of the derived class constructor. In *timezone.h,* these are the same because the **TimeZone** constructor is an **inline** function. But when the derived class's constructor is not an **inline** function, the base constructor's argument list does not appear in the derived class definition. Instead, it appears in the declaration of the constructor function as follows:

```
// ------- class definition
class TimeZone : public Time {
  // ...
public:
  // ---- constructor function definition
  TimeZone(int, int, int, timezone);
};
// ------ constructor function declaration
TimeZone::TimeZone(int hr, int min, int sec, timezone zn)
                         : Time(hr, min, sec)
{
  // ...
}
```

The arguments to the constructor function of the base class are expressions that may use constants and the parameter list of the derived class's constructor function. They can be any valid C++ expressions that match the types of the base constructor's parameter list.

When a base class has more than one constructor function, the compiler will decide which one to call based on the types of the arguments in the base constructor argument list as specified by the derived class constructor function.

Overriding Members in the Derived Class

When a base and a derived class have public member functions with the same name and parameter list types, the function in the derived class overrides that in the base class when the function is called as a member of the derived class object.

Both the base **Time** class and the derived **TimeZone** class have functions named **display**. A program that declares an object of type **TimeZone** can call the **display** function for that type, and the function in the derived class object executes.

Exercise 9-3 is a program that uses the derived **TimeZone** class.

```
#include "timezone.h"

main()
{
    TimeZone tz(10, 26, 0, est);
    tz.display();
}
```

Exercise 9-3 — Using a Derived Class.

By including *timezone.h*, the program has everything it needs to use the **TimeZone** class. If any of the **Time** or **TimeZone** member functions were not **inline**, the program would also need to link to the object files that contained those functions.

Exercise 9-3 displays the following message:

`10:26:0 EST`

A program can declare objects of both the base and derived classes. The two objects are independent of one another.

Exercise 9-4 shows a program that uses **Time** and **TimeZone** objects.

```
#include <iostream.h>
#include "timeday.h"
#include "timezone.h"

main()
{
    Time tm(23, 15, 45);
    tm.display();
    cout << '\n';
    TimeZone tz(10, 26, 0, est);
    tz.display();
}
```

Exercise 9-4 — Using a Base and a Derived Class.

Exercise 9-4 displays the following messages showing that each object uses the **display** function of its own class:

```
23:15:45
10:26:0 EST
```

Classes Derived from Derived Base Classes

You can derive a class from a base class that was itself derived from another base class. Suppose that neither the **Time** class nor the **TimeZone** class fully satisfies a new requirement.

The **Time** class maintains the 24-hour military clock. (Actually, it records and displays whatever value you care to write into the hour with your initializers. A more complete class might validate its initializers.) But suppose there is a new requirement to display the time in a 12-hour format with the time zone indicator and with am or pm notation. You can derive a class from the **TimeZone** base that incorporates the new requirements.

Exercise 9-5 is *disptime.h*, a header source file that defines the **DispTime** class that is derived from the **TimeZone** class.

```
// ---------- disptime.h

#ifndef DISPTIME_H
#define DISPTIME_H

#include <stdio.h>
#include "timezone.h"

//
// A DispTime Class
//
```

Exercise 9-5 continued...

...from previous page

```
inline int adjust(int hour)
{
    return hour > 12 ? hour - 12 : (hour == 0 ? 12 : hour);
}

inline char makeampm(int hour)
{
    return hour < 12 ? 'a' : 'p';
}

class DispTime     : public TimeZone {
protected:
    char ampm;
public:
    DispTime(int hr, int min, int sec, timezone zn)
            : TimeZone(adjust(hr), min, sec, zn)
        { ampm = makeampm(hr); }
    void display()    {
        Time::display();
        cout << ' ' << ampm << 'm';
        cout << ' ' << TZ [zone];
    }
};

#endif
```

Exercise 9-5 — Header to Define Derived **DispTime** *Class.*

The exercise begins with two **inline** functions. The first, **adjust**, adjusts the 0 to 24 hour value to one that is correct for a 12-hour clock. Zero becomes 12, and 13 to 23 become 1 to 11. The second **inline** function, **makeampm**, returns the letter *a* if the hour is less than 12, otherwise it returns *p*.

> This use of **inline** functions shows how the **inline** keyword can replace the preprocessor's **#define** statement for macros with parameters. The **inline** format is better because it enjoys all the notational convenience of a function declaration.

Note that the argument list for the base **TimeZone** constructor uses the **adjust** function to initialize the **hours** data member all the way up in the base **Time** class. When you use the **DispTime** class, **hours** will always be 1 to 12.

The **DispTime** constructor initializes the **ampm** data member by calling the **makeampm** function with the **hr** parameter as an argument.

> The class definitions for **TimeZone** and **DispTime** both make their private members protected. The class definition for **Time** did not. This circumstance reflects what you are likely to run into when you deal with classes from other sources. A designer of a derived class is sensitive to how a base class definition can help the process. If you needed the data members from the **Time** class to be protected, you could always change the header file that defines **Time**. This is not a good practice. It is not wise to change code that might be in use elsewhere even if the change appears to be unobtrusive.

Exercise 9-6 is a program that uses the **DispTime** class.

```
#include "disptime.h"

main()
{
    DispTime dt(21, 42, 12, pst);
    dt.display();
}
```

Exercise 9-6 — Using a Derived Class from a Derived Class.

Exercise 9-6 initializes the object with a 24-hour clock value and uses the class's display function to **display** the following message:

```
9:42:12 pm PST
```

Pointers to Base and Derived Classes

The three classes, **Time**, **TimeZone**, and **DispTime**, represent three generations in a straight line of inheritance. They also all three have functions named **display** that perform differently. You can use these characteristics to observe how C++ behaves with class inheritance.

A pointer to a base class can be assigned the address of one of the base's derived class objects. If the derived class overrides members of the base, the compiler associates operations made through that pointer to the base class components of the object. This means that if a derived class member overrides a base class member, the pointer will ignore the override.

Exercise 9-7 is a program that has a single object of type **DispTime** and three pointers to classes, one to each of the three types.

```cpp
#include <iostream.h>
#include "disptime.h"

main()
{
    DispTime dt(21, 42, 12, pst);
    Time     *tp = &dt;
    TimeZone *zp = &dt;
    DispTime *dp = &dt;
    tp->display();
    cout << '\n';
    zp->display();
    cout << '\n';
    dp->display();
}
```

Exercise 9-7 — Pointers to Base and Derived Classes.

Exercise 9-7 displays the following messages showing that the compiler selects the member function based on the type of the pointer rather than on the type of the object:

```
21:42:12
21:42:12 PST
9:42:12 pm PST
```

Global Scope Resolution Operator with Base and Derived Classes

A program can use the **::** global scope resolution operator to bypass the override of a member that a derived class has overridden.

Exercise 9-8 declares an object of type **DispTime** and a pointer to same.

```cpp
#include <iostream.h>
#include "disptime.h"

main()
{
    DispTime dt(21, 42, 12, pst);
    DispTime *dp = &dt;

    // -------- use the DispTime display function
    dp->display();
    cout << '\n';
    dt.display();
    cout << '\n';
```

Exercise 9-8 continued...

...from previous page

```
    // -------- use the TimeZone display function
    dp->TimeZone::display();
    cout << '\n';
    dt.TimeZone::display();
    cout << '\n';

    // -------- use the Time display function
    dp->Time::display();
    cout << '\n';
    dt.Time::display();
    cout << '\n';
}
```

Exercise 9-8 — Global Scope Resolution in Base and Derived Classes.

Exercise 9-8 calls the **display** function of the **DispTime** class twice, once directly via the object and once through the pointer. Then it uses the **::** global scope resolution operator to specify that it intends to use the **display** function for **TimeZone**, the base class of **DispTime**. Finally, it does the same override to call the **display** function for Time (the base class of TimeZone) which is two generations removed from the object's **DispTime** class. The program displays the following messages:

```
9:42:12 pm PST
9:42:12 pm PST
21:42:12 PST
21:42:12 PST
21:42:12
21:42:12
```

References to Base and Derived Classes

A reference to a base class can be initialized with one of the base's derived class objects. If the derived class overrides members of the base, the compiler associates operations made through that reference to the base class components of the object. If a derived class member overrides a base class member, the reference will ignore the override.

Exercise 9-9 is a program that has a single object of type **DispTime** and three references to classes, one to each of the three types.

```
#include <iostream.h>
#include "disptime.h"

main()
{
    DispTime dt(21, 42, 12, pst);
    Time&     tp = dt;
    TimeZone& zp = dt;
    DispTime& dp = dt;
    tp.display();
    cout << '\n';
    zp.display();
    cout << '\n';
    dp.display();
}
```

Exercise 9-9 — References to Base and Derived Classes.

Exercise 9-9 displays the same messages as Exercise 9-7 showing that the compiler selects the member function based on the type of the reference rather than on the type of the object.

Virtual Functions

A virtual function is one that is defined in a base class and that expects to be overridden by a function in a derived class with the same name and parameter types. You saw earlier that when a pointer to a base class points to a derived class object, a call to an overridden function through the pointer calls the function that is a member of the base class rather than the one belonging to the object. A virtual function will, on the other hand, pass the calls to it to the matching function that is declared in a derived class when the call is made from an object of the derived class. This is true regardless of the type of the pointer or reference that calls the function.

Time Classes with Virtual Functions

Exercise 9-10 uses *times.h*, a header file that modifies the three time classes, to make the display function virtual.

```
// ---------- times.h

#ifndef TIMES_H
#define TIMES_H

#include <iostream.h>
#include <stdio.h>

//
// A Time Class
//

class Time    {
    int hours, minutes, seconds;
public:
    Time(int hr, int min, int sec)
        { hours = hr; minutes = min; seconds = sec; }
    virtual void display()
        { cout << hours << ':' << minutes << ':' << seconds; }
};

//
// A TimeZone Class
//
enum timezone { gmt, est, cst, mst, pst };
char *TZ[] = { "GMT", "EST", "CST", "MST", "PST" };
```

Exercise 9-10 continued...

...from previous page

```
class TimeZone    : public Time {
protected:
    timezone zone;
public:
    TimeZone(int hr, int min, int sec, timezone zn)
            : Time(hr, min, sec)
        { zone = zn; }
    virtual void display()
        { Time::display(); cout << ' ' << TZ [zone]; }
};


//
// A DispTime Class
//

inline int adjust(int hour)
{    return hour > 12 ? hour - 12 : (hour == 0 ? 12 : hour); }

inline char makeampm(int hour)
{    return hour < 12 ? 'a' : 'p'; }

class DispTime    : public TimeZone {
protected:
    char ampm;
public:
    DispTime(int hr, int min, int sec, timezone zn)
            : TimeZone(adjust(hr), min, sec, zn)
        { ampm = makeampm(hr); }
    void display()    {
        Time::display();
        cout << ' ' << ampm << 'm';
        cout << ' ' << TZ [zone];
    }
};

#endif
```

Exercise 9-10 — Header File to Redefine the **Time** *Classes with Virtual Functions.*

The three classes in *times.h* are identical to those in *timeday.h*, *timezone.h* and *disptime.h* except that the **display** functions of the **Time** and **TimeZone** class are virtual.

Exercise 9-11 is the same program as that in Exercise 9-9, except that it includes *times.h* instead of *disptime.h*; therefore, it uses the newer definitions for the classes.

```
#include <iostream.h>
#include "times.h"

main()
{
    DispTime dt(21, 42, 12, pst);
    Time&     tp = dt;
    TimeZone& zp = dt;
    DispTime& dp = dt;
    tp.display();
    cout << '\n';
    zp.display();
    cout << '\n';
    dp.display();
}
```

Exercise 9-11 — Reference to a Virtual Function.

Exercise 9-11 displays the following messages:

```
9:42:12 pm PST
9:42:12 pm PST
9:42:12 pm PST
```

When you compare these messages with those displayed by Exercise 9-9, you can see that the compiler now elects to use the **display** function in the **DispTime** class even when the reference is to the type **Time** or **TimeZone**. The behavior with pointers is the same.

Overriding the Virtual Function Override

If you want a virtual function to execute even when the calling object has an overriding function, you can use the **::** global scope resolution operator to specify that the virtual function is to execute.

Exercise 9-12 modifies the program from Exercise 9-11 so that the virtual **TimeZone.display** function executes, even though the **DispTime** object has an overriding **display** function. The modified program displays the same messages as Exercise 9-9.

```
#include <iostream.h>
#include "times.h"

main()
{
    DispTime dt(21, 42, 12, pst);
    Time&     tp = dt;
    TimeZone& zp = dt;
    DispTime& dp = dt;
    tp.Time::display();
    cout << '\n';
    zp.TimeZone::display();
    cout << '\n';
    dp.display();
}
```

Exercise 9-12 — Overriding the Virtual Function Override.

Virtual Functions without Derived Overrides

If the derived class has no function to override the base class's virtual function, then the base class's function will execute regardless of the pointer or reference type.

Exercise 9-13 uses the class definitions of **Time** and **TimeZone** to demonstrate that a virtual function in a base class will execute if the derived class of the invoking object has no overriding function.

```
#include <iostream.h>
#include <stdio.h>

//
// A Time Class
//
class Time    {
    int hours, minutes, seconds;
public:
    Time(int hr, int min, int sec)
        { hours = hr; minutes = min; seconds = sec; }
    virtual void display()
        { cout << hours << ':' << minutes << ':' << seconds; }
};


//
// A TimeZone Class
//
enum timezone { gmt, est, cst, mst, pst };

class TimeZone    : public Time {
protected:
    timezone zone;
public:
    TimeZone(int hr, int min, int sec, timezone zn)
            : Time(hr, min, sec)
        { zone = zn; }
};

main()
{
    TimeZone dt(21, 42, 12, pst);
    Time&     tp = dt;
    tp.display();
    cout << '\n';
    dt.display();
}
```

Exercise 9-13 — Virtual Function with no Derived Override.

The **TimeZone** class in Exercise 9-13 has no **display** function to override the virtual **display** function of the **Time** class. Therefore, both calls to the **display** function execute the virtual function in the **Time** class, and the program displays the following messages:

```
21:42:12
21:42:12
```

Pure Virtual Functions

A base class can specify a pure virtual function, which means that the base class will not provide a declaration of the function. In this case, the program may not declare any objects of the base class and the derived class must either declare the function or define it also as a pure virtual function to be declared at an even lower level in the class hierarchy.

The following code shows you how to specify a pure virtual function with an initializer to zero in its definition in the class:

```
class Time {
  // ...
public:
    virtual void display() = 0;
}
```

Exercise 9-14 modifies the program in Exercise 9-13 by specifying a pure virtual **display** function for the **Time** class and by replacing the **display** function in the **TimeZone** class.

```
#include <iostream.h>
#include <stdio.h>

// ------------- A Time Class
class Time    {
protected:
    int hours, minutes, seconds;
public:
    Time(int hr, int min, int sec)
        { hours = hr; minutes = min; seconds = sec; }
    virtual void display() = 0;
};

// ------------ A TimeZone Class
enum timezone { gmt, est, cst, mst, pst };
char *TZ[] = { "GMT", "EST", "CST", "MST", "PST" };

class TimeZone    : public Time {
protected:
    timezone zone;
public:
    TimeZone(int hr, int min, int sec, timezone zn)
            : Time(hr, min, sec)
        { zone = zn; }
    void display();
};

void TimeZone::display()
{
    cout << hours << ':' << minutes << ':'
        << seconds << ' ' << TZ [zone];
}
```

Exercise 9-14 continued...

... from previous page

```
main()
{
    TimeZone dt(21, 42, 12, pst);
    Time&     tp = dt;
    tp.display();
    cout << '\n';
    dt.display();
}
```

Exercise 9-14 — Pure Virtual Function.

Exercise 9-14 displays the following messages:

```
21:42:12 PST
21:42:12 PST
```

> C++ Version 2.1 removes the requirement that there be a path of pure virtual functions from the one in the highest base class down to a function with the same name and parameter list in a derived class. Each lower derived class inherits the pure virtual function of a base class. Somewhere in the class hierarchy between the base class and the class of a declared object there must exist a function that has the same name and parameter list as the pure virtual function.

Virtual Functions and Multiple Derived Classes

If a base class has more than one derived class and more than one of them overrides a virtual function, the compiler will select the function from the class for which the calling object is declared.

Exercise 9-15 defines an abstract **Date** class and two derived classes, **NumDate** and **AlphaDate**. The **Date** class has a pure virtual function named **display** that is overridden by **display** functions in the derived classes.

```
#include <iostream.h>

// --------- abstract date class
class Date {
protected:
    int mo, da, yr;
public:
    Date(int m, int d, int y) {mo = m; da = d; yr = y;}
    virtual void display() = 0;
};

// --------- derived numeric date class
class NumDate : public Date {
public:
    NumDate(int m, int d, int y) : Date(m, d, y)
        { /* ... */ }
    void display()
    { cout << mo << '/' << da << '/' << yr; }
};

// -------- derived alphabetic date class
class AlphaDate : public Date {
public:
    AlphaDate(int m, int d, int y) : Date(m, d, y)
        { /* ... */ }
    void display();
};
```

Exercise 9-15 continued...

...from previous page

```
// ------ Display function for AlphaDate
void AlphaDate::display()
{
    static char *mos[] = {
        "January","February","March","April","May","June",
        "July", "August","September","October","November",
        "December"
    };
    cout << mos[mo-1] << ' ' << da << ", " << yr+1900;
}

main()
{
    NumDate nd(7,29,41);
    AlphaDate ad(11,17,41);

    Date& dt1 = nd;
    Date& dt2 = ad;
    dt1.display();
    cout << '\n';
    dt2.display();
}
```

Exercise 9-15 — Virtual Functions and Multiple Derived Classes.

The program in Exercise 9-15 declares objects of types **NumDate** and **AlphaDate**. The two dates have different initialized values so you can tell them apart. Then the program declares two references to **Date** objects, initializing one to refer to the **NumDate** object and the other to refer to the **AlphaDate** object. The important point is that both references as defined refer to the base class, but as initialized they refer to the derived class objects.

The program calls the **display** function by using the **Date** references and displays the following messages:

```
7/29/41
November 17, 1941
```

When the program calls the **display** function through a reference to the **Date** class, the compiler must select a function to execute. Because the **display** function in the **Date** class is virtual, the compiler selects the **display** function for the object to which the **Date** reference refers.

The Virtue of the Virtual Function

In the next exercise you have a string of base and derived classes like the following:

OrgEntity – Company – Division – Department

OrgEntity is the root base and **Department** is the lowest derived class. The **OrgEntity** class is an abstract class, which means its sole purpose is to be a base class. It has a function named **number_employees**, and every class in the hierarchy has a virtual function named **office_party**. The functions return the variable number of employees assigned to each organizational entity and a constant amount per employee budgeted for the annual office party. The lower an entity is in the organization, the less money is budgeted per employee for the party.

Exercise 9-16 is *org.h*, the header file that defines these four base and derived classes.

```
// ------------ org.h

#ifndef COMPANY_H
#define COMPANY_H

#include <iostream.h>
#include <string.h>

class OrgEntity {
    char name[25];
    int employee_count;
```

Exercise 9-16 continued...

...from previous page

```
public:
    OrgEntity(char *s, int ec)
        { strcpy(name, s); employee_count = ec; }
    int number_employees() { return employee_count; }
    char *org_name() { return name; }
    virtual int office_party() = 0;
};

class Company : public OrgEntity    {
public:
    Company(char *s, int ec) : OrgEntity(s, ec) { }
    virtual int office_party() { return 100; }
};

class Division : public Company    {
public:
    Division(char *s, int ec) : Company(s, ec) { }
    virtual int office_party() { return 75; }
};

class Department : public Division    {
public:
    Department(char *s, int ec) : Division(s, ec) { }
    int office_party() { return 50; }
};

#endif
```

Exercise 9-16 — An Organization's Class Structure.

It might appear that the three lower classes in *org.h* could each simply derive from the **OrgEntity** base class. So they could, but, while not shown in the exercise, in actual practice such classes would contain other specialized and inherited members related to the organizational entities they represent. Tiered layers of inheritance would, therefore, be appropriate.

Somewhere in the organization's accounting system is a budget management process that generates annual budget reports. It does not necessarily know what kind of organizational entity it is working with at the time so it must rely on the design of the class hierarchy to cause each class to behave in its own unique way.

Exercise 9-17 is a program that emulates this relationship. The main function stubs the exercise by declaring objects of the classes and calling the **budget** function for each one.

```cpp
#include <iostream.h>
#include "org.h"

void budget(OrgEntity& oe);

main()
{
    Company company("Bilbo Software, Inc.", 35);
    Division div("Vertical Applications", 12);
    Department dept("Medical Practice", 4);
    budget(company);
    budget(div);
    budget(dept);
}

void budget(OrgEntity& oe)
{
    cout << "\n---- Budget Report ----\n";
    cout << oe.org_name();
    cout << " $" << oe.number_employees() * oe.office_party();
    cout << '\n';
}
```

Exercise 9-17 — A Company's Budget Program.

The **budget** function represents a part of a software system that does not necessarily know which of the classes derived from **OrgEntity** it is dealing with. The virtual **office_party** function represents a way that each derived class can provide its own specialized behavior for a given process. The program displays the following messages:

```
---- Budget Report ----
Bilbo Software, Inc. $3500
---- Budget Report ----
Vertical Applications $900
---- Budget Report ----
Medical Practice $200
```

This ability for each derived class to provide its own custom version of a general function and for the compiler to select the correct one based on the object being processed, is called *polymorphism* in the object-oriented lexicon.

Destructors in Base and Derived Classes

When an object of a derived class goes out of scope, the destructor for the derived class executes and then the destructor for the base class executes. There is an opportunity for a problem in this scheme, however. If the destructor executes as the result of the **delete** operator and if the pointer type is the base class, the base destructor will execute instead of the derived destructor.

Exercise 9-18 illustrates this destructor-execution behavior in base and derived classes.

```
#include <iostream.h>
#include <string.h>

class Company  {
    char *name;
public:
    Company(char *s)
        { name = new char[strlen(s)+1]; strcpy(name, s); }
    ~Company() { cout << "\nC destructor"; delete name; }
    void org_name() { cout << name; }
};

class Division : public Company  {
    char *manager;
public:
    Division(char *s, char *mgr) : Company(s)
    {manager=new char[strlen(mgr)+1]; strcpy(manager, mgr);}
    ~Division() {cout << "\nD destructor"; delete manager;}
};

main()
{
    Company *companies[3];
    companies[0] = new Company("Bilbo Software, Inc.");
    companies[1] = new Division("Vert Apps", "Ron Herold");
    companies[2] = new Division("Horiz Apps", "Bob Young");
    for (int i = 0; i < 3; i++)    {
        // ....... process the company objects
        delete companies[i]; // not always right destructor
    }
}
```

Exercise 9-18 — Base and Derived Destructors.

When you design a hierarchy or network of classes, you must consider each method with respect to whether or not it should be a virtual function. If you are defining a member function whose method is specific to the class, you must ask if any derived class might have a similar function with the same name. The **display** function you have seen in many exercises in this book is a good example of a general-purpose function whose operation could be overridden by a derived class. Next you must ask whether calls of the function will always be in the name of the actual object or whether it might be through a pointer or reference to a base class. Answering that, you must determine whether such calls need the services of the function that is a member of the pointer/reference class or whether they need a virtual function that will find its way to the member function of the actual class of which the object is a type. These are the kinds of decisions that face the designer of an object-oriented class network.

Exercise 9-18 has a base **Company** class and a derived **Division** class. Both classes have destructors because they both contain pointer data members that are initialized with free store-memory by their constructors.

The destructor functions of both classes display messages to show that they are executing, and they both **delete** the free store memory to which their member pointers point.

The main function declares an array of pointers to the **Company** class, initializes one of them with a pointer to a new **Company** object, and initializes the other two with pointers to new **Division** objects. Because these objects were built by the **new** operator, they must be destroyed by the **delete** operator.

The main function uses a **for** loop to process and delete the objects. But because the pointers in the array are **Company** types, the **delete** operator calls the destructor function for the **Company** class even when the pointer points to a **Division** object. The result is that the free store memory allocated to the two **Division** class objects for their **manager** members never gets deleted. Exercise 9-18 displays the following messages to prove that only the **Company** destructor ever gets called:

```
C destructor
C destructor
C destructor
```

The solution to the problem presented by Exercise 9-18 is to declare the destructor function for the base class to be virtual. When a base class destructor is virtual, all the destructors below it in the hierarchy are automatically virtual, and the compiler can call the correct destructor function.

Exercise 9-19 is the same as Exercise 9-18, except that the destructor function in the base Company class is virtual.

Note that while destructor functions can be virtual, constructor functions cannot.

```cpp
#include <iostream.h>
#include <string.h>

class Company  {
    char *name;
public:
    Company(char *s)
        { name = new char[strlen(s)+1]; strcpy(name, s); }
    virtual ~Company()
        { cout << "\nC destructor"; delete name;}
    void org_name() { cout << name; }
};

class Division : public Company  {
    char *manager;
public:
    Division(char *s, char *mgr) : Company(s)
    {manager=new char[strlen(mgr)+1]; strcpy(manager, mgr);}
    ~Division() { cout << "\nD destructor"; delete manager;}
};

main()
{
    Company *companies[3];
    companies[0] = new Company("Bilbo Software, Inc.");
    companies[1] = new Division("Vert Apps", "Ron Herold");
    companies[2] = new Division("Horiz Apps", "Bob Young");
    for (int i = 0; i < 3; i++)    {
        // ....... process the company objects
        delete companies[i]; // always right destructor
    }
}
```

Exercise 9-19 — Virtual Destructor.

Exercise 9-19 displays the following messages:

```
C destructor
D destructor
C destructor
D destructor
C destructor
```

The first **C destructor** message comes when the program deletes the **Company** object. The next two pairs of messages, **D destructor**, **C destructor**, come when the program deletes the two **Division** objects.

Multiple Inheritance

Multiple inheritance is the ability for a derived class to have more than one base class. Its purpose is to allow you to define a new class that inherits the characteristics of multiple, but otherwise unrelated, base classes.

There are a few notational differences in the use of multiple base classes. First is the way you specify more than one base class when you define the derived class. You would use the following notation to define a **FileStamp** class that derived from both the **Time** class and the **Date** class:

```
class FileStamp : public Time, public Date {
    // ...
};
```

The constructor function declaration in a class that is derived from multiple bases must specify the arguments for the constructors of all the base classes. The following notation is for such a constructor function:

```
FileStamp::Filestamp(int dd,int mm,int yy,
                     int hr,int mn,int sc)
    : Time(hr, mn, sc), Date(mm, dd, yy)
```

Exercise 9-20 is a program that derives the **FileStamp** class from two bases, the **Time** class and the **Date** class. In this exercise, the **FileStamp** class is one that records the date and time when something happens to a file. It has its own data member to store the name of the file, and it uses the properties it inherits from the **Date** and **Time** classes to manage the date and time.

```cpp
#include <iostream.h>
#include <string.h>

// ------ base Time class
class Time {
protected:
    int hours, minutes, seconds;
public:
    Time(int h, int m, int s)
        { hours = h; minutes = m; seconds = s; }
    virtual void display()
        { cout << hours << ':' << minutes << ':' << seconds; }
};

// ------ base Date class
class Date {
protected:
    int month, day, year;
public:
    Date(int m, int d, int y)
        { month = m; day = d; year = y; }
    virtual void display()
        { cout << month << '/' << day << '/' << year; }
};
```

Exercise 9-20 continued...

...from previous page

```
// ------ derived FileStamp class
class FileStamp : public Time, public Date    {
protected:
    char filename[15];
public:
    FileStamp(char *fn, int mm, int dd, int yy,
                      int hr, int mn, int sc)
              : Time(hr, mn, sc), Date(mm, dd, yy)
        { strcpy(filename, fn); }
    void display();
};

// ----- the display function for the derived class
void FileStamp::display()
{
    cout << filename << ' ';
    Date::display();
    cout << ' ';
    Time::display();
}

main()
{
    FileStamp fs("DATAFILE", 4, 6, 90, 13, 32, 27);
    fs.display();
}
```

Exercise 9-20 — Multiple Inheritance.

The **Date** and **Time** classes each have **display** functions to display their contents. The **FileStamp** function overrides those functions with its own **display** function. The **FileStamp::display** function uses the virtual **display** functions of the two base classes by using the **::** global scope resolution operator to call them.

Exercise 9-20 displays the following message:

```
DATAFILE 4/6/90 13:32:27
```

Ambiguities with Multiple Inheritance

Suppose that the **FileStamp** class in Exercise 9-20 had no **display** function to override the virtual **display** functions of the two base classes. This would not be a problem as long as the program did not attempt to call the **display** function through an object of type **FileStamp**, or a pointer or references to one. If it did, however, the program would not compile because the compiler would not know which of the two **display** functions to execute. The program can resolve this ambiguity by using the **::** global scope resolution operator to specify which class's **display** function to use, as shown in the following example:

```
fs.Date::display();
```

The same ambiguities can exist with data members. If both base classes have data members with the same name and the derived class has no such data member, the member functions of the derived class must use the **::** global scope resolution operator to resolve which base class's data member to use.

If the data members are public, the program cannot access such an ambiguous data member directly through the object, but must use the global scope resolution operator and the base class name in the same manner that is shown for member functions above.

Constructor Execution with Multiple Inheritance

When the program declares an object of a class that is derived from multiple bases, the constructors for the base classes are called first. The order of execution is the order in which the base classes are declared as bases to the derived class. Consider the following example:

```
class FileStamp : public Time, public Date {
    // ...
};
```

The constructor for the **Time** class executes first followed by the constructor for the **Date** class with the constructor for the **FileStamp** class coming last.

If the class definition includes another class as a member, that class's constructor executes after the constructors for the base classes and before the constructor for the class being defined. Consider the following example:

```
class Name { /* ... */ };
class FileStamp : public Time, public Date {
    Name filename;
    // ...
};
```

The order of constructor execution is **Time**, **Date**, **Name**, and **FileStamp**.

Destructor Execution with Multiple Inheritance

When an object of a class goes out of scope, the destructors execute in the reverse order of the constructors.

Virtual Base Classes

With multiple inheritance there is the opportunity for a derived class to have too many instances of one of the bases. Consider the following structure:

```
class BillingItem {
protected:
    char name[25];
    int cost;
public:
    virtual void display() = 0;
};
```

The **BillingItem** class is an abstract class that will be the base class for two derived classes in a system that supports the sale of products and services. The following are the derived classes:

```
class Product : public BillingItem {
protected:
    int qty_sold;
public:
    Product(char *nm, int qty, int cst)
        { qty_sold = qty; }
    void display() { cout << qty_sold; }
};
class Service : public BillingItem {
protected:
    int manhours;
public:
    Service(char *nm, int mh, int cst)
        { manhours = mh; }
    void display() { cout << manhours; }
};
```

A program that declares an object of either of these classes has access to the **name** and **cost** data members of the base **BillingItem** class. That, combined with the **display** functions of the derived classes, gives the program the ability to report the details of individual product and service sales.

Suppose that the system also needs to support the sale of installed products where the sale involves a number of products and the labor hours to perform the installation. It is reasonable to want to build a new class that inherits the characteristics of the two existing classes. Such a new class is shown as follows:

```
class Installation : public Product, public Service   {
public:
    Installation(char *nm, int qty, int hrs, int cst)
        : Product(nm, qty, cst), Service(nm, hrs, cst)  { }
    void display();
};
```

A problem arises because the **Product** and **Service** classes are both derived from the **BillingItem** class, therefore, the **Installation** class will inherit two copies of it. You do not want that to happen. An installation is one billing item with one name and one cost.

It does not need two representations of these data members. Furthermore, any attempt to address **name** or **cost** for an **Installation** object would result in an ambiguity that the program could resolve only by applying the **::** scope resolution operator to associate the member with one of the intermediate base classes.

C++ allows you to specify in the definition of a derived class that a base class is virtual. The result will be that all virtual occurrences of the class throughout the class network will share one actual occurrence of it. To specify a virtual base class, use the following notation:

```
class Product : public virtual BillingItem {
    // ...
};
```

There are rules, however, about how a virtual base class can itself be specified. A class that uses a constructor that accepts parameters cannot be a virtual base class. If this restriction did not exist, the compiler would not know which constructor argument list from which derived class to use. Note that a pointer to a virtual base class cannot be cast to a class that is derived from it, either directly or further down the class network.

Exercise 9-21 shows the use of a virtual base class such as the one just discussed.

```
#include <iostream.h>
#include <string.h>

class BillingItem    {
protected:
    char name[25];
    int cost;
public:
    virtual void display() = 0;
};

class Product : public virtual BillingItem    {
    int qty_sold;
public:
    Product(char *nm, int qty, int cst)
        { qty_sold = qty; strcpy(name, nm); cost = cst; }
    void display() { cout << qty_sold; }
};

class Service : public virtual BillingItem    {
    int manhours;
public:
    Service(char *nm, int mh, int cst)
        { manhours = mh; strcpy(name, nm); cost = cst; }
    void display() { cout << manhours; }
};

class Installation : public Product, public Service    {
public:
    Installation(char *nm, int qty, int hrs, int cst)
        : Product(nm, qty, cst), Service(nm, hrs, cst) { }
    void display();
};
```

Exercise 9-21 continued...

…from previous page

```
void Installation::display()
{
    cout << "\nInstalled ";
    Product::display();
     cout << ' ' << name << 's';
    cout << "\nLabor: ";
    Service::display();
    cout << " hours";
    cout << "\nCost: $" << cost;
}

main()
{
    Installation inst("refrigerator", 2, 3, 75);
    inst.display();
}
```

Exercise 9-21 — Virtual Base Classes.

Both the **Product** and the **Service** class definitions specify that the **BillingItem** base class is virtual. Observe that the constructors for these two classes take care of initializing the data members for the **BillingItem** class because it cannot have a constructor with a parameter list. The **Installation** class is derived from the **Product** and **Service** classes.

The main function declares an **Installation** object, initializes it with some values, and uses its **display** function to display the following messages:

```
Installed 2 refrigerators
Labor: 3 hours
Cost: $75
```

Summary

This chapter is the end of the tutorial exercises with which you taught yourself C++. You now know enough about the language to use it in the design and development of some complex and interesting programs.

However, there is more to know about the C++ language development environment. Along with implementations of the language comes a library of standard stream input/output classes and functions. You have already used that library extensively by including *iostream.h* in the exercises and using the **cin** and **cout** objects to read and write the console. Chapter 10 is about C++ input/output streams and how you can use their advanced features for file input/output as well as for the console.

Chapter 10

Advanced C++ Input/Output Streams

T he exercises in this book have used the C++ **iostream** class library to read input from the keyboard and display results on the screen. The **iostream** class library has capabilities beyond those that read and write the console, however. The library is the C++ equivalent to the standard C stream input/output functions, and you can use it to manage console and file input/output. This chapter discusses some of the advanced capabilities of the **iostream** class library.

The **iostream** classes have more features than this chapter describes. After mastering the usages in the exercises given here, you should refer to the **iostream** documentation that comes with your compiler to see how to use its more advanced features. This chapter provides sufficient knowledge to use the streams in the ways that support most programming problems.

C++ has no input/output operators as intrinsic or integral parts of the language. Just as C relies on function libraries to extend the language with input/output functions, C++ depends on class libraries for its input and output.

Versions of C++ prior to 2.0 included the **stream** class library, and that library is documented in Stroustrup's *The C++ Programming Language.* (See the bibliography at the end of this book.) Some of the books that predate version 2.0 of C++ also deal with the earlier **stream** classes only.

C++ Version 2.0 uses the improved **iostream** class library. Version 2.0 compilers also include support for the **stream** library so that programs developed with earlier versions are compatible with the newer compiler. Those programs included the *stream.h* header file while users of 2.0 include *iostream.h* and others to use the improved classes.

The Zortech compiler does not support the newer **iostream** libraries, using instead their own improved version of the older **stream** library. This book does not describe the Zortech implementation. Most of the exercises in earlier chapters work with the old and new stream libraries and will, therefore, work with the Zortech compiler. This chapter addresses only the standard **iostream** facilities.

Some compilers support both generations of **stream** classes from within the *iostream.h* header file. Those compilers use the *stream.h* file name as an alias for the *iostream.h* name so that older programs will compile without modification. Other compilers provide both header files.

C++ manages file and console input and output as streams of characters. C++ programs manage data values as data types such as integers, structures, classes, etc. The **iostream** library provides the interface between the data types that a program views and the character streams of the input/output system.

Most of the exercises in this book include the *iostream.h* header file. You can learn a lot about the design of class networks by reading this file. You can also answer some of your own questions about the use of the streams by looking at how they are implemented in the file.

Streams

Chapter 1 introduced the C++ **iostream** class library and showed some of the ways to use it. That introduction was to allow you to proceed with the exercises in this book, most of which use console input/output. Without knowing about C++ classes, you were not prepared to fully understand how the classes and their objects were implemented. Now that you have classes, overloaded operators, and inheritance under your belt, you are prepared to learn more about how to use the features of the **iostream** libraries.

The *ios* Class

C++ streams are implemented as classes. The **cout** and **cin** objects are instances of those classes, all of which derive from a base class named **ios**. There is not much to know about **ios** except when coding **enum** values that **ios** defines. A program deals mostly with objects of types that are derived from the **ios** class.

The *ostream* Class

Stream output is managed by a class named **ostream**, which derives from **ios**. You learned to display a message on the screen with a statement such as the following one:

```
cout << "Hello, Dolly";
```

The **cout** object is an external object of the **ostream** class. The **cout** object is declared in the library, and an **extern** declaration of it appears in *iostream.h* so that it is available to be used by any program that includes *iostream.h*.

Besides **cout**, *iostream.h* declares other objects as instances of the **ostream** class. The **cerr** object writes to the standard error device and uses unbuffered output. The **clog** object also writes to the standard error device but it uses buffered output. A later part of this chapter describes buffered output.

A program writes to an **ostream** object by using the << insertion operator. The exercises in this book have used this feature extensively. The **ostream** class provides sufficient overloaded << insertion operators to support writing most standard C++ data types. Later you will learn how to overload the << insertion operator to write your own classes to an **ostream** object.

The *istream* Class

The **istream** class manages stream input the way the **ostream** class manages output. It is externally declared in *iostream.h*. The **cin** object reads data values from the standard input device.

The **istream** class uses the **>>** extraction operator to read input. There are sufficient overloaded extraction **>>** operators to support reading the standard C++ data types, and a user-defined class can overload the **>>** extraction operator to read data from an **istream** object. You will learn how to do this later.

The *iostream* Class

The **iostream** class is derived from the **istream** and **ostream** classes. A program would use it for the declaration of objects that do both input and output. You do not often need to deal with the **iostream** class in basic input/output operations. The **fstream** class, which manages file input/output, derives from the **iostream** class, and that is as close as most programmers will need to come to **iostream**.

Buffered Output

The data characters written to an **ostream** object are usually buffered. For example, the **ostream** class collects output bytes into a buffer and does not write them to the actual device associated with the object until the one of the following events occurs: the buffer fills, the program tells the object to flush its buffer, the program terminates, or, if the output object is **cout**, the program reads data from the **cin** object. The **cout** and **clog** objects use buffered output. The **cerr** object does not.

Exercise 10-1 displays a "please wait" message, which does some extensive processing—in this case just a five-second wait loop — and then proceeds.

```
#include <iostream.h>
#include <time.h>

main()
{
    time_t tm = time((time_t *)NULL) + 5;
    cout << "Please wait...";
    while (time((time_t *)NULL) < tm)
        ;
    cout << "\nAll done";
}
```

Exercise 10-1 — A Buffered Stream Object.

The "please wait" message does not always display when it should, because **cout** is a buffered object. The solution is to tell cout to flush itself as soon as you want the message to display. A program tells an **ostream** object to flush itself by sending it the **flush** manipulator.

Exercise 10-2 uses the **flush** manipulator to cause the program in Exercise 10-1 to work the way it is intended.

```
#include <iostream.h>
#include <time.h>

main()
{
    time_t tm = time((time_t *)NULL) + 5;
    cout << "Please wait..." << flush;
    while (time(NULL) < tm)
        ;
    cout << "\nAll done";
}
```

Exercise 10-2 — Flushing a Buffered Stream.

Formatted Output

Chapter 1 included discussions on the **dec**, **oct**, and **hex** manipulators. These manipulators set the default format for input and output. If you insert the **hex** manipulator into the output stream, for example, the object correctly translates the internal data representation of the object into the correct display. Exercise 1.6 in Chapter 1 demonstrated this behavior.

Output width

Objects of type **ostream** write data without padding as a default. The exercises in this book insert the space character between data values in the output stream to separate them. You might want some displays to be lined up in columns, which means that displays need to be written with a fixed width.

A program can specify a default width for every item displayed by inserting the **setw** manipulator into the stream or by calling the **width** member function. The **setw** manipulator and the **width** member function both take a width parameter.

Exercise 10-3 is a program that displays a column of numbers.

```
#include <iostream.h>

main()
{
    cout.unsetf(ios::scientific);
    cout.setf(ios::fixed);
    static double values[] = { 1.23, 35.36, 653.7, 4358.224 };
    for (int i = 0; i < 4; i++)
        cout << values[i] << '\n';
}
```

Exercise 10-3 — Displaying Columns of Numbers.

Exercise 10-3 displays the following output:

```
1.23
35.36
653.7
4358.224
```

Observe the calls to the **unsetf** and **setf** member functions for the **cout** object. These calls clear and set flags that are related to the object and that control output format. The **scientific** flag, which this exercise clears, formats a **double** or **float** output with exponential notation. The **fixed** flag formats the output with decimal positions. The default for the **iostream** library that accompanies C++ Version 2.0 is a fixed format. The default for 2.1 is scientific. These two statements are not necessary with 2.0.

Exercise 10-4 demonstrates how the **width** member function manages output width. By calling the **width** function with an argument of 10, the program specifies that the displays are to appear in a column at least 10 characters wide.

```
#include <iostream.h>

main()
{
    cout.setf(ios::fixed, ios::scientific);
    static double values[] = { 1.23, 35.36, 653.7, 4358.224 };
    for (int i = 0; i < 4; i++)    {
        cout.width(10);
        cout << values[i] << '\n';
    }
}
```

Exercise 10-4 — The **width** *Member Function.*

Exercise 10-4 displays the following output:

```
      1.23
     35.36
     653.7
  4358.224
```

The **setf** call in Exercise 10-4 differs from the one in Exercise 10-3. This variation on the call has two parameters, the flag to set and a mask that defines the flags to clear.

Sometimes a report needs to use different widths for different data elements, and it is convenient to insert width commands into the stream. The **setw** manipulator provides this capability.

Exercise 10-5 demonstrates the use of the **setw** manipulator to display columns that have data elements with different width requirements.

```
#include <iostream.h>
#include <iomanip.h>

main()
{
    cout.setf(ios::fixed, ios::scientific);
    static double values[] = { 1.23, 35.36, 653.7, 4358.224 };
    static char *names[] = {"Zoot", "Jimmy", "Al", "Stan"};
    for (int i = 0; i < 4; i++)
        cout << setw(6)  << names[i]
                << setw(10) << values[i] << '\n';
}
```

*Exercise 10-5 — The **setw** Manipulator.*

You must include *iomanip.h* to use the **setw** manipulator.

Exercise 10-5 displays the following output:

```
  Zoot      1.23
 Jimmy     35.36
    Al     653.7
  Stan  4358.224
```

Note that using **setw** or **width** does not cause any truncation. If the data value being displayed is wider than the current width value, the entire data value still displays. You should be aware of this behavior when you design well-formatted displays that use the **setw** manipulator or the **width** member function.

Note also that the default width you specify applies only to the object for which you specified it and not for other objects of the class.

To return the object to the default width, use the **width** member function or the **setw** manipulator with a zero argument.

You can use the **fill** member function to set the value of the padding character for output that has other than the default width.

Exercise 10-6 demonstrates this usage by padding a column of numbers with asterisks.

```
#include <iostream.h>

main()
{
    cout.setf(ios::fixed, ios::scientific);
    static double values[] = { 1.23, 35.36, 653.7, 4358.224 };
    for (int i = 0; i < 4; i++)     {
        cout.width(10);
        cout.fill('*');
        cout << values[i] << '\n';
    }
}
```

*Exercise 10-6 — The **fill** Member Function.*

Exercise 10-6 displays the following output:

```
******1.23
*****35.36
*****653.7
**4358.224
```

Output Justification

Suppose that you want the names in Exercise 10-5 to be left-justified and the number to remain right-justified. You can use the **setiosflags** manipulator to specify that the output is to be left or right justified.

Exercise 10-7 demonstrates **setiosflags** by modifying the display from Exercise 10-5 so that the names are left justified.

```
#include <iostream.h>
#include <iomanip.h>

main()
{
    cout.setf(ios::fixed, ios::scientific);
    static double values[] = { 1.23, 35.36, 653.7, 4358.224 };
    static char *names[] = {"Zoot", "Jimmy", "Al", "Stan"};
    for (int i = 0; i < 4; i++)
        cout << setiosflags(ios::left)
             << setw(6)  << names[i]
             << resetiosflags(ios::left)
             << setiosflags(ios::right)
             << setw(10) << values[i] << '\n';
}
```

Exercise 10-7 — The **setiosflags** *and* **resetiosflags** *Manipulators.*

Exercise 10-7 displays the following output:

```
Zoot         1.23
Jimmy       35.36
Al          653.7
Stan     4358.224
```

The exercise sets the left justification flag by using the **setiosflags** manipulator with an argument of **ios::left**. This argument is an **enum** value that is defined in the **ios** class, so its reference must include the **ios::** prefix. The **resetiosflags** manipulator turns off the left justification flag to return to the default right justification mode.

Precision

Suppose you wanted the floating point numbers in Exercise 10-7 to display with only one decimal place. The **setprecision** manipulator tells the object to use a specified number of digits of precision.

Exercise 10-8 adds the **setprecision** manipulator to the program.

```
#include <iostream.h>
#include <iomanip.h>

main()
{
    static double values[] = { 1.23, 35.36, 653.7, 4358.224 };
    static char *names[] = {"Zoot", "Jimmy", "Al", "Stan"};
    for (int i = 0; i < 4; i++)
        cout << setiosflags(ios::left)
             << setw(6)
             << names[i]
             << resetiosflags(ios::left)
             << setiosflags(ios::right)
             << setw(10)
             << setprecision(1)
             << values[i]
             << '\n';
}
```

Exercise 10-8 — The **setprecision** *Manipulator.*

Exercise 10-8 displays the following output:

```
Zoot          1.2
Jimmy        35.4
Al         6.5e+02
Stan       4.4e+03
```

The scientific notation displayed by Exercise 10-8 might not be what the program needs to display. There are two flags, **ios::fixed** and **ios::scientific**, that control how a floating point number displays. A program can set and clear these flags with the **setiosflags** and **resetiosflags** manipulators.

Exercise 10-9 uses the **setiosflags** manipulator to set the **ios::fixed** flag so that the program does not display in scientific notation.

```
#include <iostream.h>
#include <iomanip.h>

main()
{
    static double values[] = { 1.23, 35.36, 653.7, 4358.224 };
    static char *names[] = {"Zoot", "Jimmy", "Al", "Stan"};
    for (int i = 0; i < 4; i++)
        cout << setiosflags(ios::left)
            << setw(6)
            << names[i]
            << resetiosflags(ios::left)
            << setiosflags(ios::fixed)
            << setiosflags(ios::right)
            << setw(10)
            << setprecision(1)
            << values[i]
            << '\n';
}
```

Exercise 10-9 — Setting the **ios::fixed** *Flag.*

Exercise 10-9 displays the following output:

```
Zoot         1.2
Jimmy       35.4
Al         653.7
Stan      4358.2
```

Manipulators, Flags, and Member Functions

The exercises in this discussion have used manipulators and member functions to change the various modes of display, which are controlled by flags. The **ios** class keeps the current settings of the flags in member data items. The class defines the mnemonic values for the settings in an **enum** data type. Many of the modes can be changed with both a manipulator and a member function. Which one you use depends on how convenient it might be for the display at hand. Some of the mode changes remain in place until you change them again. Others reset themselves to their default values after every output message.

At the time this book is being written, the **iostream** class library is relatively new. Different compiler vendors have implemented it according to their own interpretations of the AT&T specification. As a general rule, the implementations are consistent because most implementors use the AT&T source code as a baseline.

Input/Output Member Functions

There are several member functions associated with the **ostream** and **istream** classes that perform input and output. These member functions are alternatives to the extraction and insertion operators providing better ways to manage certain kinds of input and output.

Output Member Functions

put

The **put** member function writes a single character to the output stream. The following two statements are the same:

```
cout.put('A');
cout << 'A';
```

write

The **write** member function writes any block of memory to the stream in binary format. Because **write** does not terminate when it sees a null it is useful for writing the binary representations of data structures to stream files, which are discussed later.

Exercise 10-10 illustrates the **write** function with the **cout** object.

```
#include <iostream.h>

main()
{
    static struct    {
        char msg[23];
        int alarm;
        int eol;
    } data = { "It's Howdy Doody time!", '\a', '\n' };

    cout.write( (char *) &data, sizeof data);
}
```

*Exercise 10-10 — The **ostream write** Function.*

In Exercise 10-10, the message is displayed. The program will write the message, sound the alarm and advance to the next line.

Note the cast to **char*** before the address of the structure object. The **write** function accepts **char** pointers and **unsigned char** pointers only. The address of the structure must be cast to one of these.

Input Member Functions

The **>>** extraction operator has a limitation that programs sometimes need to overcome: The extraction operator bypasses white space. If you type characters on a line that is being read by the extraction operator, only the non-space characters come into the receiving character variable. The spaces are skipped. Likewise, if the program uses the extraction operator to read a string of words, the input stops when it finds a space character. The next word is read into the next (if any) use of the extraction operation on the **istream** object, and all spaces between the words are lost.

The **istream** class includes the **get** and **getline** member functions to handle reading input characters that must include white space.

get

The **get** member function works just like the **>>** extraction operator except that white space characters are included in the input.

Exercise 10-11 demonstrates the difference between the two operations.

```
#include <iostream.h>

main()
{
    char line[25], ch = 0, *cp;

    cout << " Type a line terminated by 'x'\n>";
    cp = line;
    while (ch != 'x')    {
        cin >> ch;
        *cp++ = ch;
    }
    *cp = '\0';
    cout << ' ' << line;

    cout << "\n Type another one\n>";
    cp = line;
    ch = 0;
    while (ch != 'x')    {
        cin.get(ch);
        *cp++ = ch;
    }
    *cp = '\0';
    cout << ' ' << line;
}
```

Exercise 10-11 — The **istream get** *Member Function.*

In Exercise 10-11, two strings are read from the keyboard one character at a time. The first input uses the extraction operator and the second one uses the **get** member function. If you typed "now is the timex" for both entries, the screen would look like the following display:

```
Type a line terminated by 'x'
>now is the timex              (entered by you)
 nowisthetimex                 (echoed by the program)
 Type another one
>now is the timex              (entered by you)
 now is the timex              (echoed by the program)
```

You can see that the extraction operator skips over the white space and the **get** function does not. The program needs the **x** terminator because it needs to know when to stop reading. Because **cin** is a buffered object, the program does not begin to start seeing characters until you type the carriage return, and that character is not seen by the program.

A variation of the **get** function allows a program to specify a buffer address and the maximum characters to read.

Exercise 10-12 shows how the **get** function can specify a buffer address and length, instead of a character variable to receive the input.

```
#include <iostream.h>

main()
{
    char line[25];
    cout << " Type a line terminated by carriage return\n>";
    cin.get(line, 25);
    cout << ' ' << line;
}
```

Exercise 10-12 — Using **get** *with a Buffer and Length.*

Exercise 10-12 reads whatever you type into the structure and echoes it to the screen.

The length value minus one is the maximum characters that will be read into the buffer. You can type more than that number but the excess characters are not kept.

getline

The **getline** function works the same as the variation of the **get** function demonstrated in Exercise 10-12. Both functions allow a third argument that specifies the terminating character for input. If you do not include that argument, its default value is the newline character.

Exercise 10-13 uses the **getline** function with a third argument to specify a terminating character for the input stream.

```
#include <iostream.h>

main()
{
    char line[25];
    cout << " Type a line terminated by 'q'\n>";
    cin.getline(line, 25, 'q');
    cout << ' ' << line;
}
```

Exercise 10-13 — The **istream getline** *Member Function.*

If you type "after this I quit," the program screen will look like the following:

```
Type a line terminated by 'q'
after this I quit          (entered by you)
after this I               (echoed by the program)
```

read

The **istream** class's **read** member function is the input equivalent of the **write** function. It reads the binary representation of the input data into the buffer without bypassing white space. It is usually used with file input/output described later.

Exercise 10-14 is an example of using the **read** function to read a string of characters from the keyboard into a structure.

```
#include <iostream.h>

main()
{
    struct    {
        char msg[23];
    } data;

    cin.read( (char *) &data, sizeof data);
    cout << data.msg;
}
```

Exercise 10-14 — The **istream read** *Function.*

Exercise 10-14 reads whatever you type into the structure and echoes it to the screen.

Overloading the << Insertion and >> Extraction Operators

The overloaded insertion and extraction operators work with the standard C++ data types. A user-defined class can overload them to work with the data formats of the class itself making a program more readable. It is clearer when a program can use the second of the following two statements:

```
dt.display(); // call a member function to display the object
cout << dt;   // send the dt object to the cout object
```

The second statement is also more flexible as you will soon see. The overloaded insertion operator can work with **ostream** objects other than just **cout**. Similarly, the overloaded extraction operator can work with **istream** objects other than just **cin**. You might, for example, display a class on the **cerr** stream or write it to a file.

Overloading <<

Consider the **Date** class that the exercises in this book have used extensively. Usually the **Date** class in an exercise also has a **display** member function that sends the data members to the **cout** object in a date format. The following is a more intuitive way to display a class object:

```
Date dt(1,2,88);
cout << dt;
```

To get the **cout** object to accept a **Date** object along with the insertion operator, the program must overload the insertion operator to recognize an **ostream** object on the left and a **Date** on the right. The overloaded << operator function must then be a friend in the **Date** class definition so that it could get to the private data members of the **Date**.

Exercise 10-15 overloads the << insertion operator with an **iostream** object on the left and a **Date** object on the right.

```cpp
#include <iostream.h>

class Date {
    int mo, da, yr;
public:
    Date(int m, int d, int y) { mo = m; da = d; yr = y; }
    friend ostream& operator<< (ostream& os, Date& dt);
};

ostream& operator<< (ostream& os, Date& dt)
{
    os << dt.mo << '/' << dt.da << '/' << dt.yr;
    return os;
}

main()
{
    Date dt(5, 6, 77);
    cout << dt;
}
```

Exercise 10-15 — Overloading the << Operator.

253

Exercise 10-15 displays the date 5/6/77 on the screen.

Overloading >>

Overloading the >> extraction operator allows a class to have an intelligent class input function that knows about the input requirements of the class's data members.

Exercise 10-16 is an example of overloading the extraction operator to read a date into the **Date** class.

```
#include <iostream.h>

class Date {
    int mo, da, yr;
public:
    Date() {}
    friend ostream& operator<< (ostream& os, Date& dt);
    friend istream& operator>> (istream& is, Date& dt);
};

ostream& operator<< (ostream& os, Date& dt)
{
    os << dt.mo << '/' << dt.da << '/' << dt.yr;
    return os;
}

istream& operator>> (istream& is, Date& dt)
{
    is >> dt.mo >> dt.da >> dt.yr;
    return is;
}

main()
{
    Date dt;
    cout << "Enter a date (mm dd yy): ";
    cin >> dt;
    cout << dt;
}
```

Exercise 10-16 — Overloading the >> Operator.

Exercise 10-16 displays a date that you enter as shown here.

```
Enter a date (mm dd yy): 6 29 90
6/29/90
```

The overloaded >> operator in the exercise has the user type the three components of a date with intervening spaces. The overloaded >> operator in **istream** skips white space, so the **Date** overloaded >> operator function uses that feature to collect three integers from **cin**. You might prefer to read the date into a string with intervening slashes or dashes and then use the C **atoi** function to parse the values into the **Date** class data members. A complete date input function would certainly validate the values for the month, day, and year.

File Input/Output

A file stream is an extension of a console stream. File stream classes are derived from the console stream classes and inherit all the characteristics of the console. But files have some requirements of their own that character devices such as the console do not have. Files have distinct names. A program can append data to an existing file. A program can seek to a specified position in a file. The class inheritance facility of C++ is a natural way to build file classes from console classes, and that is how the file stream classes work.

A program that uses the file stream classes must include the *fstream.h* header file where the classes are defined. The program might also include *iostream.h*, but it is not necessary because *fstream.h* itself includes *iostream.h*.

The *ofstream* Class

The **ofstream** class objects are files that a program can write to. In the most elementary use of **ofstream**, the program declares an object of type **ofstream**, gives it a name, and writes to it. When the object goes out of scope the file closes.

Exercise 10-17 uses an **ofstream** object in its simplest form.

```
#include <fstream.h>

main()
{
    ofstream tfile("test.dat");
    tfile << "This is test data";
}
```

Exercise 10-17 — File Output.

The program creates a file and writes a string to it.

You can use the **ofstream** class to append to an existing file.

Exercise 10-18 illustrates appending to a file by appending a string to the file that Exercise 10-17 created.

```
#include <fstream.h>

main()
{
    ofstream tfile("test.dat", ios::app);
    tfile << ", and this is more";
}
```

Exercise 10-18 — Appending to an Output File.

The **write** member function works well with **ofstream** classes.

Exercise 10-19 shows how the **write** function can record the binary representation of a class object into a data file.

```
#include <fstream.h>

class Date    {
    int mo, da, yr;
public:
    Date(int m, int d, int y) { mo = m; da = d; yr = y; }
};

main()
{
    Date dt(6, 24, 40);
    ofstream tfile("date.dat");
    tfile.write((char *) &dt, sizeof dt);
}
```

Exercise 10-19 — The **write** *Member Function.*

The program creates the file and writes the binary value of the **Date** object into it. The **write** function does not stop writing when it reaches a null character, so the complete class structure is written regardless of its content.

The *ifstream* Class

The **ifstream** class objects are input files. A program can declare an input file stream object and read it. A program can use the **>>** extraction operator, the **get** function, or the **getline** function just as if the stream were the console device rather than a file. A program can also use the **read** member function to read binary blocks into memory.

Exercise 10-20 is a program that reads the **Date** object from the file written by Exercise 10-19.

```
#include <fstream.h>

class Date    {
    int mo, da, yr;
public:
    Date() { }
    friend ostream& operator<< (ostream& os, Date& dt);
};

ostream& operator<< (ostream& os, Date& dt)
{
    os << dt.mo << '/' << dt.da << '/' << dt.yr;
    return os;
}

main()
{
    Date dt;
    ifstream tfile("date.dat");
    tfile.read((char *) &dt, sizeof dt);
    cout << dt;
}
```

*Exercise 10-20 — The **read** Member Function.*

Exercise 10-20 displays the date 6/24/40 on the screen.

Streams have a number of status bits that reflect the current state of the stream. The values of the bits are defined in an **enum** in the **ios** class, and there are member functions that can test and change the bits. The **eof** member function returns a true value if the stream has reached the end of its character stream.

Exercise 10-21 reads a text file a character at a time, sending each character to **cout** and stopping at end-of-file.

```
#include <fstream.h>

main()
{
    ifstream tfile("test.dat");
    while (!tfile.eof())    {
        char ch;
        tfile.get(ch);
        cout << ch;
    }
}
```

Exercise 10-21 — Testing End-of-File.

Exercise 10-21 displays this message:

```
This is test data, and this is more
```

259

Seeking

Disk drives are random access devices. Therefore, disk files must be capable of random access. A program can modify the current position of a file stream by using one of the member functions **seekg** which changes the position of the next input operation or **seekp** which changes the position of the next output operation.

Exercise 10-22 opens a file, changes the input position, and then reads to end of file.

```
#include <fstream.h>

main()
{
    ifstream tfile("test.dat");
    tfile.seekg(5);          // seek five characters in
    while (!tfile.eof())     {
        char ch;
        tfile.get(ch);
        cout << ch;
    }
}
```

*Exercise 10-22 — The **seekg** Member Function.*

Exercise 10-22 displays this message:

```
is test data, and this is more
```

A program can specify that a **seekg** or **seekp** operation occur relative to the beginning of the file, the end of the file, or the current position by adding an argument to the function call. The argument is defined in an **enum** in the **ios** class. The following are examples of the function calls:

```
tfile.seekg(5, ios::beg);
tfile.seekg(10, ios::cur);
tfile.seekg(-15, ios::end);
```

If you do not provide the second argument, the seek occurs from the beginning of the file.

You can determine the current position for input with the **tellg** member function and the current position for output with the **tellp** member function.

Exercise 10-23 illustrates the **tellg** function.

```
#include <fstream.h>

main()
{
    ifstream tfile("test.dat");
    while (!tfile.eof())     {
        char ch;
        streampos here = tfile.tellg();
        tfile.get(ch);
        if (ch == ' ')
            cout << "\nPosition " << here << " is a space";
    }
}
```

Exercise 10-23 — The **tellg** *Function.*

Exercise 10-23 displays these messages.

```
Position 4 is a space
Position 7 is a space
Position 12 is a space
Position 18 is a space
Position 22 is a space
Position 27 is a space
Position 30 is a space
```

The program reads the file built by earlier exercises and displays messages showing the character positions where it finds spaces. The **tellg** function returns an integral value of type **streampos**, a **typedef** defined in *iostream.h*.

The *fstream* Class

The **fstream** class supports file stream objects that a program opens for both input and output. Typical examples are data base files where a program reads records, updates them, and writes them back to the file.

An object of type **fstream** is a single stream with two logical substreams, one for input and one for output. Each of the two substreams has its own position pointer. The pointers follow each other. There are two pointers because they are defined in the **ifstream** and **ofstream** classes and are available to objects of those classes as well.

Files opened in append mode always write to the end of the file. They also change the input position pointer to just past the last character after every write.

Exercise 10-24 is a program that reads the text file from the earlier exercises into a character array and writes an uppercase only copy of the bytes at the end of the file.

```
#include <fstream.h>
#include <ctype.h>

main()
{
    fstream tfile("test.dat", ios::in | ios::app);
    char tdata[100];
    int i = 0;
    while (!tfile.eof())
        tfile.get(tdata[i++]);
    tfile.clear();
    for (int j = 0; j < i; j++)
        tfile.put(toupper(tdata[j]));
}
```

Exercise 10-24 — An **fstream** *File.*

The program must include the call to the **clear** member function before starting the writes because the stream is at end-of-file. The **clear** member function clears the end-of-file and all other indicators, and that allows the program to proceed with the output.

Opening and Closing a Stream File

A program can declare an **ifstream**, **ofstream**, or **fstream** object without a name. When it does, the object exists, but no file is associated with it. You must then use the **open** member function to associate a file with the **fstream** object. You can disassociate the file from the object by calling the **close** member function. This technique allows a single object to represent different files at different times.

Exercise 10-25 demonstrates the use of the **open** function to associate the stream object with a file and the **close** function to disassociate the object from a file.

```
#include <fstream.h>

main()
{
    ofstream tfile;    // an ofstream object without a file
    tfile.open("test1.dat");
    tfile << "This is TEST1";
    tfile.close();
    tfile.open("test2.dat");
    tfile << "This is TEST2";
    tfile.close();
}
```

*Exercise 10-25 — **open** and **close** Member Functions.*

The **iostream** classes include conversion functions that return true or false values if you use the object name in a true/false conditional expression. Suppose you declare a file stream object without an initializing name and do not associate a name with that object. The following code shows how you might test for that condition:

```
fstream tfile;    // no file name given
if (tfile)        // this test will return false
    // ...
```

How to Open a File

The C and C++ stream facilities for opening files are less than instantly intuitive. Veteran programmers still have to stop and think when they are about to open a file. Does the file already exist? May the file already exist? If the file already exists should the program truncate it? Append to it? If the file does not exist should the program create it? The variations on this theme go on and on.

The **open** member function and the implied open operation performed by the constructor take an **open_mode** integer value as a parameter. The argument values for the **open_mode** parameter are defined in the **ios** class. You optionally provide one or more of these parameters in a logical OR expression depending on how you want the file to be opened.

Here is a list of the **open_mode** bits defined in the **ios** class.

ios::app Append to an output file. Every output operation is performed at the physical end of file, and the input and output file pointers are repositioned immediately past the last character written.

ios::ate The **open** operation includes a seek to the end of the file. This mode can be used with input and output files.

ios::in This is an input file and is an implied mode for **ifstream** objects. If you use **ios::in** as an **open_mode** for an **ofstream** file, it prevents the truncation of an existing file.

ios::out This is an output file and is an implied mode for **ofstream** objects. When you use **ios::out** for an **ofstream** object without **ios::app** or **ios::ate**, **ios::trunc** is implied.

ios::nocreate The file must exist, otherwise the **open** fails.

ios::noreplace The file must not exist, otherwise the **open** fails.

ios::trunc Delete the file if it already exists and re-create it.

There are seven of these bits. There are three types of objects, **ofstream**, **ifstream**, and **fstream**. Therefore there are 381 possible open statements for you to code. Not all of them would be logical, but you could code them all. For each of them, the file might exist or it might not. Therefore, there are 762 possible circumstances. Covering them all is beyond the scope of this book. However, here are some of the most common circumstances:

1. You want to create a file. If it exists, delete the old one.

```
ostream ofile("FILENAME");  // no open_mode
```

2. You want to read an existing file. If it does not exist, an error has occurred.

```
istream ifile("FILENAME");  // no open_mode
if (ifile.fail())
    // the file does not exist ...
```

3. You want to read and write an existing file. This is an update mode. You might read records, seek to records, rewrite existing records, and add records to the end of the file.

```
fstream ffile("FILENAME", ios::in | ios::out | ios::nocreate);
if (ffile.fail())
    // the file does not exist ...
```

4. You want to write to an existing file without deleting it first.

```
ofstream ofile("FILENAME", ios::in);
```

5. You want to append records to an existing file, creating it if it does not exist.

```
ofstream ofile("FILENAME", ios::out | ios::app);
```

Testing Errors

A program can and should test errors when it uses input/output file streams. Each stream object has its own set of condition flags that change according to the current state of the object. You already used one of these flags when you tested for end-of-file with the **eof** member function. Other member functions that test for flag settings are **bad**, **fail**, and **good**. The **bad** function returns a true value if your program attempts to do something illegal such as seek beyond the end of the file. The **fail** function returns a true value for all conditions that include the **bad** positive return plus any valid operations that fail such as trying to open an unavailable file or trying to write to a disk device that is full. The **good** function returns true whenever **fail** would return false.

Exercise 10-26 attempts and fails to open a nonexisting file for input.

```
#include <fstream.h>

main()
{
    ifstream ifile;
    ifile.open("noname.fil", ios::in | ios::nocreate);
    if (ifile.fail())
        cout << "Cannot open";
    else    {
        // ...
        ifile.close();
    }
}
```

Exercise 10-26 — File Error Checking.

Exercise 10-26 displays the "Cannot open" message on the screen.

Note the use of the **ios::nocreate** mode value as an argument to the **open** member function. This argument tells the **open** function to fail if the file does not exist. Therefore, the call to the **fail** member function returns true because the file does not exist. This function works the same way whether you open the file with the **open** member function or specify the file name as an initializer in the declaration of the stream object.

Summary

The C++ Stream Library has many other features and facilities. For example, there is a set of classes that support in-memory formatting much like the **sprintf** and **sscanf** functions of C but with all the insertion and extraction operations and member functions of the **iostream** classes.

With the introduction in this chapter you have learned how to use C++ stream classes as they apply to most input/output applications. After you have used them for a while you might want to read the description of their advanced features in the documentation that accompanies your compiler.

Chapter 11

What's Next?

C++ has a strong future. Many compiler vendors, library vendors, and programmers are committed to its success. Dr. Stroustrup has proposed two language additions that the X3J16 committee is considering. These changes support parameterized data types and exception handling. Both recommendations are in the experimental stage and are not implemented in formal releases of C++ compilers.

Parameterized Data Types

Parameterized data types are templates that allow you to describe a data type that supports the management of another data type. Typical uses for parameterized types would be to build general-purpose container classes, such as lists and queues, and database file managers that do not themselves specify the data type that they will manage.

Consider the **ListEntry** linked list class that you used in Exercises 7-20 and 7-24. These linked lists managed lists of character pointers. A program might need several linked lists, with each one managing a different data type.

With parameterized data types, you could define a general-purpose linked-list class template with an unspecified data type as a parameter. You could then define classes that associated the template with a specified data type.

The format of a template specification is proposed to be as shown in this example:

```
template<class ListEntry> class LinkedList {
    ListEntry *p;
public:
    // ...
    void AddEntry(ListEntry &);
};
```

The template specifies that you can declare objects of type **LinkedList** with a parameter that specifies the data type to be managed by the list. The **ListEntry** identifier represents the parameterized data type throughout the definition. The identifier can be any acceptable C++ data type including classes of your own design. You could therefore declare two different linked lists, as shown here:

```
LinkedList<char *> CharList;
LinkedList<Date> DateList;
```

These statements declare two **LinkedList** objects with different properties. The first one is a list of character pointers. The second one is a list of a classes named **Date** that you have defined elsewhere.

You must provide template functions for the member functions of a parameterized data type. The fragmented linked list example given here includes a function to add an entry to the list. You would declare the function as shown here:

```
template<class ListEntry>
    void LinkedList<ListEntry>::AddEntry(ListEntry &le)
{
    // ...
}
```

You would then add an entry to the character pointer list with this call:

```
CharList.AddEntry("New data added to the list");
```

A template can contain more than one data type parameter, making it possible to build parameterized data types of considerable complexity.

The definition of the parameterized data type is still in progress, and the details are not final. The discussion given here is based on the original proposal, which is far from complete and which contains a number of suppositions and alternatives. The ANSI X3J16 committee is still working on the proposal. When it is completed and implemented in C++ compilers, this ability will be a strong addition to the C++ language.

Exception Handling

When exception handling becomes a part of C++, it will be the C++ analogue to ANSI C's **signal** and **raise**. Exception handling is a way to allow a program to intercept errors and transfer control outside the block in which the error occurred without requiring the program to clean up its own environment. Many C programs perform similar operations by using **longjmp**. C++ has more far-reaching requirements than **longjmp** because there might be layers of class destructors that need to be executed, and some of these destructors might be partial if the error occurs within a class constructor or destructor.

C++ functions that can sense and recover from errors execute from within a **try** block that looks like this:

```
try  {
    // C++ statements
}
```

The **try** block is followed by a **catch** exception handler with a parameter list as shown here:

```
catch(Date dt)   {
    // error-handling code
}
```

There can be multiple **catch** handlers with different parameter lists.

To intercept an error and pass control to a **catch** handler, a C++ function issues the **throw** statement with a data type that matches the parameter list of the proper **catch** handler list this:

```
throw Date(da, mo, yr);
```

This example assumes that there is a class named **Date** that can be constructed with the **da**, **mo**, **yr** parameter list. The **throw** statement builds a temporary object of type **Date** and initializes the object with the values given in the **throw** statement. Then **throw** cleans up all objects declared within the **try** block by calling their destructors. Next, **throw** cleans up the stack and the free store, restoring them to their condition at the time the **try** block was entered. Finally, **throw** executes the matching **catch** handler, passing to **catch** the temporary object that **throw** created. The following code fragment brings it all together:

```
void f()
{
    // C++ statements
    throw Date(da, mo, yr);
}
try  {
    f();
}
catch(Date dt)   {
    // error-handling code
}
```

The proposal for C++ exception handling does not make it clear whether the **throw** statement can be in the **try** block itself or only in functions called directly or indirectly from within the **try** block.

You can throw an object declared ahead of the throw statement, even if the object is automatic and the handler expects a reference, like this:

```
void f()
{
    // C++ statements
    throw Date(da, mo, yr);
}
try  {
    f();
}
catch(Date& dt)    {
    // error-handling code
}
```

This technique will work because the **throw** statement builds a temporary variable to throw.

You can specify the exceptions that a function may **throw** when you declare the function as shown here:

```
void f() throw(Date)
{
    // C++ statements
    throw Date(da, mo, yr);
}
```

If a function includes an exception-specification as shown above, and the function **throw**s an exception not given in the specification, the exception is passed to a system function named **unexpected()**. The **unexpected** function calls the latest function named as an argument in a call to the **set_unexpected** function, which returns its current setting.

A **catch** with ellipses for a parameter list as shown next list will catch all exceptions:

```
catch(...)   {
    // error-handling code
}
```

You can code a **throw** with no operand in a **catch** handler or in a function called by one. This notation will pass the exception being handled to the next **catch** handler in the list as shown here:

```
catch(Date dt)   {
    // partial error-handling code
    throw;   // pass the exception to the next catch
}
catch(Time tm)   {
    // more error-handling code
}
```

Summary

This chapter taught you about parameterized data types and exception handling, two proposed additions to the C++ language.

C++ is under your belt now. You know enough about C++ to begin working with it in earnest. Many of you will use one of the compilers in the Appendix. C++ is new enough that no two compilers are the same, even those that are ports of the AT&T licensed version. The programs in this book are as close as possible to all the implementations. Some of them do not compile with all the compilers, but the warnings and error messages will tell you what to change to make the code compatible with your compiler.

You should begin reading about, experimenting with, and learning about object oriented programming now. Your new knowledge of C++ gives you the tools to build complex object-oriented systems, and that combination will be the programming platform of choice in the decade to come.

Appendix

C++ Compilers for MS-DOS Computers

Following is a discussion of C++ 2.0 compilers that users of MS-DOS computers can purchase as this book is being written. This list has changed since the first edition of this book and will surely grow with time.

Borland C++ 2.0

Borland International, Inc.
1800 Green Hills Road
PO Box 660001
Scotts Valley, CA 95066-0001
(408) 438-5300

Borland C++ is a compiler implementation of C++ 2.0. Borland C++ was originally packaged as Turbo C++ 1.0, but Borland modified the emphasis of their marketing to align the version number with the AT&T release and to add support for programming under Microsoft Windows 3.0.

Comeau C++

Comeau Computing
91-34 120th Street
Richmond Hill, NY 11418
(718) 945-0009

Comeau C++ is a CFRONT port, which means that it is an adaptation of the AT&T C++ 2.1 translator to run under MS-DOS and UNIX. The CFRONT program reads your C++ source code and translates it into C code which must be compiled by a C compiler. You will need a copy of Microsoft C to compile the translated output from Comeau C++.

TopSpeed C++

Jensen & Partners, Inc.
1101 San Antonio Road, Suite 301
Mountain View, CA 94043
(800) 543-5202

TopSpeed C++ is a compiler that implements C++ version 2.1. The compiler is one part of a multiple-language product that includes C, C++, Pascal, and Modula 2. The languages share a common code generator and integrated development environment.

Zortech C++ 2.1

Zortech Incorporated
1165 Massachusetts Avenue
Arlington, MA 02174
(617) 646-6703

Zortech C++ uses the 2.1 version number, but does not incorporate the AT&T 2.1 changes. Zortech's input/output stream classes and libraries are different than the iostreams described in Chapter 10. Few, if any, of those exercises work with Zortech

C++. Other exercises in the book do not work with Zortech C++ because of some differences in the way Zortech built their C++ compiler. The explanations that accompany such exercises will tell you that the exercises do not work properly with Zortech C++.

Glossary

This glossary defines some terms that have specific meaning in the realms of C++ and object-oriented programming.

abstract data type

An object-oriented programming (OOP) term. A class definition whose sole purpose is to be a base class from which other classes can be derived. Further, no specific objects of the base class will be declared by a program. C++ implements abstract data types with the pure virtual function.

anonomous object

An internal, temporary object created by the compiler during the evaluation of an expression, or to provide something that a reference can point to when the reference is initialized by a constant.

argument

The value passed to a function. Its type must match that of the function's corresponding parameter as declared in the function's prototype. See **parameter**.

base class

A class from which other classes derive characteristics. All the characteristics of the base are inherited by the derived class

call by reference

Calling a function and passing a reference or pointer to the caller's copy of a function argument. If the called function modifies the argument, those modifications change the caller's copy.

call by value

Calling a function and passing a copy of the value of a variable as an argument. Any changes made by the called function change the called function's copy of the variable.

class

A C++ user-defined data type that may consist of data members and member functions.

class hierarchy

A system of base and derived classes where no derived class has more than one base.

class network

A system of base and derived classes with multiple inheritance. Derived classes may have more than one base.

constructor

The function executed by the compiler when the program declares an instance of a class. See **destructor**.

conversion

See **type conversion**.

data member

A data component of a class. It may be any valid data type including class objects and references.

declaration

A statement that declares the existence of an object. A declaration reserves memory, as opposed to **definition**.

definition

A statement that defines the format of an object. A definition reserves no memory, as opposed to **declaration**.

derived class

A class that inherits some of its characteristics from a base class.

destructor

The function executed by the compiler when a declared instance of a class goes out of scope. See **constructor**.

encapsulation

An OOP term. It means the activity of defining a class with its data members and member functions encapsulated into the definition.

extraction operator

The overloaded >> operator that reads (extracts) values from an input stream. See **insertion operator**.

free store

The C++ heap.

friend

A function that has access to the private members of a class, but that is not a member function of that class. The class definition declares the function to be a friend.

hierarchy

See **class hierarchy**.

inheritance

An OOP term. The ability for one class to inherit the characteristics of another. The inherited class is said to be derived from the base class.

inline function

A function compiled by the compiler as in-line code each time the function is called.

insertion operator

The overloaded << operator that writes (inserts) values to an output stream. See **extraction operator**.

instantiation

An OOP term. The act of declaring an object of a data type, usually a class.

linkage specification

A notation that tells the C++ compiler that a function was or is to be compiled with the linkage conventions of another language.

mangled function names

The technique used by the C++ compiler to enforce type-safe linkage. It "mangles" function names internally so that the names reflect not only the function but its parameter list types as well.

manipulator

A value that a program sends to a stream to tell the stream to modify one of its modes.

member

A component of a class, either a data member or a member function.

member function

A function component of a class, also called a "method." A member function may be virtual.

message

An OOP term. A message is the invocation of a class's member function in the name of a declared object of the class. The message is said to be sent to the object to tell it to perform its function. The message includes the function call and the arguments that accompany it.

method

An OOP term. A method is a member function of a class.

multiple inheritance

An OOP term. The ability for a derived class to inherit the characteristics of more than one base class.

network

See **class network**.

object

An OOP term. A declared instance of a data type including standard C++ data types as well as objects of classes.

OOP

An acronym for object-oriented programming.

overloaded function

A function that has the same name as one or more other functions but that has a different parameter list. The compiler selects which function to call based on the data types and number of arguments in the call.

overloaded operator

A function that executes when a C++ operator is seen in a defined context with respect to a class object.

parameter

The declaration of a data item that a function expects to be passed to it. This declaration includes the item's type and name and appears in the function's declaration block at the beginning of the function. When the parameter appears in the function's prototype, the parameter's name may be omitted. See **argument** and **prototype**.

parameter list

The list of parameter types and names in a function declaration block. Also the same list, which may exclude the names, in a function prototype.

polymorphism

An OOP term. The ability for methods in a class hierarchy to exhibit different behavior for the same message depending on the type of the object for which the method is invoked and without regard to the class type of the reference to the object.

private class members

Members of a class for which access is granted only to the class's member functions and to friend functions of the class.

protected class members

Members of a class that are private except to member functions of derived classes.

prototype

The definition of a function's name, return type, and parameter list.

public class members

Members of a class to which access is granted to all functions within the scope of the object of the class.

pure virtual function

A virtual function that must have a matching function in a derived class. A program may not declare an instance of a class that has a pure virtual function.

reference

A variable that acts as an alias to another variable. It provides the convenience of pointer passing without the necessity for pointer notation.

stream

A category of character-oriented data files or devices where the data characters exist in an input or output stream.

this

A pointer that exists in all non-static member functions. The pointer is a pointer to an object of the class. It points to the object for which the function is being executed.

type conversion

The conversion of one type to another. The compiler has built-in type conversions, and a class may define its own conversions for converting from an object of the class to another type and from another type to an object of the class.

type-safe linkage

A technique that insures that functions and function calls in separately compiled program modules use consistent parameter lists.

virtual function

A member function in a class from which other classes may be derived. If the derived class has a function with the same name and parameter list, the derived class's function is always executed for objects of the derived class. See **pure virtual function**.

Bibliography

Following is a list of the articles, books, and publications that contributed to the research for Teach Yourself C++.

AT&T *Library Manual*, C++ Stream Library, 1989

AT&T C++ *Reference Manual*, 1989

Berry, John, *C++ Programming*, 1988, Howard W. Sams & Company

Dewhurst, Stephen C. and Stark, Kathy T., *Programming in C++*, 1989, Prentice Hall

Dlugosz, John M., *Computer Language Magazine*, August 1988, The Secret of Reference Variables

Ellis, Margaret A. and Stroustrup, Bjarne, *The Annotated C++ Reference Manual*, 1990, Addison-Wesley Publishing Company

Ladd, Scott Robert, *Turbo C++ Techniques and Applications*, 1990, M&T Books

Lippman, Stanley B., *C++ Primer*, 1989, Addison-Wesley Publishing Company

Pohl, Ira, *C++ for C Programmers*, 1989, The Benjamin/Cummings Publishing Company, Inc.

Stroustrup, Bjarne, *The C++ Programming Language*, 1987, Addison-Wesley Publishing Company

Wiener, Richard S. and Pinson, Lewis J., *An Introduction to Object-Oriented Programming and C++*, 1988, Addison-Wesley Publishing Company

Index

Index

Index

U

unary minus operator   182
unary plus operator   182
unexpected   273
union   34, 68
UNIX   55
unnamed function parameter   35
unsetf   241

V

variable declarations   21
virtual   17, 93, 210
virtual base class   229
virtual base class destructor   223
virtual function   207

W

width   240, 241, 242
write   247, 257

X

X3J11   3, 26
X3J16   1, 3, 271

Z

Zortech C++   1, 12, 28, 33, 41, 105, 141,
     236